DON'T KNOCK THE SOUTHERN

For Gary

DON'T KNOCK THE SOUTHERN

George Behrend
MA, FRGS, MCIT

FIRST EDITION

Midland Publishing Limited

Copyright © 1993 George Behrend

First published in 1993 by
Midland Publishing Limited
24 The Hollow, Earl Shilton
Leicester, LE9 7NA, England.

ISBN 1 85780 003 6

Printed in England by
Redwood Press Limited, Melksham, Wiltshire.

Contents

Author's Note

There are many books about the Southern Railway, and Southern Region of British Railways, so this one, by someone who has never lived long in the Southern Railway's area proper, must be different. This is a Great Western passenger's view of the Southern. It does not cover the whole system, and your favourite piece may not be here. Some twelve million people live in the area once served by the Southern Railway, plus another ten million in London, so large numbers of people know all about the Southern, for whom Sir John Elliot, who became the Company's last General Manager, invented Public Relations in 1925. Whether all these railway authors are correct or not, I am in no position to say but the books are available for all to read, covering every aspect of the Southern, and rare is the SR branch line without its very own history book. This book is a personal reflection on the Southern, and penetrates beyond the boundaries of the Southern Railway's area. The opinions are entirely my own, though in the past I have had help from David McKenna CBE, John Nolan and Norman Norman, distinguished retired SR Officers and BR Officers, as well as those, equally distinguished, who are mentioned in the text. Mr Norman has also kindly read this book in draft form. In 1959, I had the privilege of a private interview with the late Sir John Elliot.

Nobody shouted about the Southern achievements, they left this to the Public Relations people, and devotees will debate if the SR's greatest achievement was moving the troops returned from Dunkirk, or electrification at 2½ per cent interest. In its splendid English environment of the south, south-east, and west, the SR smilingly served the best people, with handles to their names, as well as at least half a million commuters daily, and also the Royal Navy, the Army, and the Royal Air Force. Now the Channel Tunnel is at last complete, Her Majesty's Government at present refuses to invest directly in the new railways needed to take proper and full advantage of it, even though new railway investment was the way out of the last slump, in the 1930s.

Parts of this book were written some years ago, and before they died, those superb photographers Maurice Earley and Arthur Russell, made some of their photographs available to me for it. Then in 1991

Tom Ferris of Midland Publishing had the bright idea of republishing my book *Gone With Regret: Recollections of the Great Western Railway, 1922-1947*. But by the time he got round to contacting me, Jersey Artists had had the same idea and were arranging for it to be reprinted. So with Tom's encouragement, I dusted off my unpublished manuscript, decided that *Don't Knock The Southern*, like good wine, had mellowed with age, and we now offer it to an unsuspecting world for the first time.

I am grateful to Chris Leigh, lately editor of *Steam Days*, Rex Kennedy the present editor and Ian Allan Ltd for permission to quote partially from my article on the Meon Valley line, which appeared in that magazine; and to Peter Kelly, editor of *Railway Magazine* to use extracts from my account of the last run of the 'Night Ferry', which appeared shortly after the event, in 1981. With the opening of the Channel Tunnel, I am delighted that this was not 'The Last Train to Paris', even though prospective passengers have had a long thirteen year wait, for the next through train! A version of Chapter Twelve, suitable for modellers, appeared a year or so back in *Continental Modeller*, made use of here by permission of the editor Andrew Burnham.

Most of those mentioned below who in the past or present have unwittingly helped me with this book, are unaware of its existence. But first I must thank those who know about it. Thanks are particularly due to Terence Cuneo OBE and to Richard Lucraft, for permission to reproduce Terence Cuneo's painting *Winston Churchill* on the jacket. Signed Limited Edition prints are available now from Richard Lucraft Limited, 1 Barrett Street, London W1M 6DN. I am also most grateful to my friends Philip Jefford, Inspecteur-General Honoraire of the Compagnie Internationale des Wagons-Lits, of St Cloud, France, who when archivist of the company uncovered the information, now published for the first time in Chapter Four, and for kindly verifying it; and Julian Morel, lately Catering Superintendent of the Pullman Car Company Limited until its operation ceased, also for verifying Chapter Four. I also especially wish to thank my friends J. H. Price, lately the accomplished editor of *Thomas Cook European Timetable* for general help, information, suggestions and photographs, and Henry Maxwell and John Alves for general help.

Thanks are also due to Sydney Preston, Director, Information Services, BR; Mike Bowler, Promotions Officer, BR InterCity Public Affairs; David Potter, Promotions Manager, BR InterCity Public Affairs (London) for his kind permission to use the maps reproduced in the Appendices, and George Reynolds, Public Affairs Manager (Scotland), of BR InterCity Public Affairs; John Noulton, Director of Public Affairs and Tony Gueterbock, OBE, UK Public Affairs Manager, EuroTunnel; David Benson, Vice-President Channel and Solent Services, Sea Containers Limited (including Wightlink); Peter Kendall, Director of Public Affairs, and Alan Dunlop, now Sales Manager, BR European Passenger

Services Limited; Julie Mitchell, BR International's Press Officer; Andy Milne and Diane Lucas, Managers of BR Railfreight Distribution Public Affairs; Peter Mills, Press Officer, and Christine Legadère, Assistant Press Officer, of French Railways Limited, London; and to Caroline Rathbone and Beatrix Carquain, Public Relations Managers of the Venice-Simplon-Orient Express Limited, for the opportunity to check various other items. I am indebted to Nigel Harris, Editor of *Steam Railway* for his kind permission to reproduce the engine details in Appendix 'A'; and to Brian Moss, Chairman of the Southern Electric Group for the information on the main electric headcodes which is published as Appendix 'B'. Thanks for present or past help are also due to Surgeon Vice-Admiral Sir John Rawlins, KBE, RN; Sherard Manners; T. A. Benger; John Goldschmid; Hans Hanenbergh (Utrecht); Basil Coleman; Colin Graham (St. Louis, USA); Eric Crozier OBE and Nancy Evans OBE; Joan Cross CBE; Dr Mike J. Harley (Winnipeg); Brendan Martin; Alby Glatt (S-Chamf); John Hendy; Paddy Kelly; Terry Bye; Tim Robbins, Pullman Engineering Administration Manager, VSOE; Major Mike Marshall, RE (Retd); D. J. Carson; Ray Privett; D. H. Tew; Chris Elliott of Medloc Enterprises (55 Cours Jean Jaures, 34120 Pezenas, France); Roy and Elaine Hogan; Jurg Schmid (Paris); David Kirby CBE; Frank Gutteridge CBE (Geneva) and any others inadvertently omitted.

Lastly I must thank Tom Ferris of Midland Publishing for his encouragement and patience, and superb hints (the latter reflected in Chapter Eight, if you look hard enough) along with his colleagues Neil Lewis and Chris Salter for making publication possible in 1993.

Findochty,
Scotland 1993.

Chapter One

Before Setting Out

A man with a death-wish design,
Lay down on the SOUTHERN main line.
But he died of *ennui*,
For the 3.43
Didn't come till a quarter past nine!
Anon.

The Southern was different to all the other big railway companies created in the 1920s by Act of Parliament. These relied on freight, especially coal, for their money. The Southern was above all a passenger line. Freight was a secondary consideration, and the Kent Coalfield, now defunct, was small compared to others in Britain.

The Southern was hemmed in firmly by the River, which every southerner knows, means the *Thames*. It got across with great expense and considerable controversy, to terminate in the heart of London at Charing Cross, Cannon Street, Holborn Viaduct and Victoria, and also in the London & South Western Railway area, to serve more places more directly than slavishly following the River's loops.

As well as the *Thames*, the LSWR was largely hemmed in by the Great Western Railway, which had no shot-gun marriages in the 1920s, but merely absorbed a number of small lines instead. It had only one passenger starting point in London, Paddington, whereas the Southern had half a dozen main termini. The Great Western Railway and the LSWR were at odds even before the latter's first trains had run. They did almost everything totally differently, and when a choice was offered, passengers devoted their patronage to one or the other, often almost exclusively.

One company, the GWR, was above all a countryman's line. The other, the LSWR, was a Londoner's line, and its great General Manager, Sir Herbert Walker, KCB, who also became the greatest and longest serving Southern Railway General Manager, and outstanding railwayman of his generation, arrived for work in his Waterloo office, by the Bakerloo line of the Underground.

Because it carried so many passengers, the Southern had expert passengers on every single line, and the great interest in it has causedinnumerable books to be written about every aspect of its many varied activities, down to the most miniscule detail. So there is no need here to repeat its basic history all over again.

Writing learnedly about the Southern is difficult and dangerous, I know, I have done it, and all these expert people are tempted to write and tell you your book is wrong, whether or not it actually is. Luckily I had a co-author, Gary Buchanan, to help me with our book on the 'Night Ferry', and in it we wrote about other railways outside Great Britain as well, which many of these people neither knew nor cared about.

In another book, which most people forgot to notice was dedicated to the railwaymen who served it, I was accused of 'rambling all over the system', as though the readers knew all about every corner of it already – but of course that was exactly what most of the readers, especially the railwaymen, *did* know. At least this book does not go rambling all over the system, for the simple reason that I have not *been* all over the system.

I wish I knew who wrote the anonymous limerick with its very slight French flavour that so marked the real Southern Railway (even though you may find it a *bore*, not to be told what *ennui* means). The easy-going, remoter Southern was quite different to the Southern Electric, with its own map, pretending the rest was not there, with little thin 'non electric' lines running off its edge.

Dr (later Lord) Beeching decided, just like me, that the Southern had no business to be in Devon and Cornwall. It was only there, because years before the LSWR had bought the Bodmin & Wadebridge Railway, and then decided that it had better join that up to a line which stretched to Waterloo. So he got rid of it, but because Meldon Quarry is the SR's enormous source of granite, quite a bit of it in Devon is still there. The blight suffered by tourist resorts like Ilfracombe and Bude, which were served by their very own portions of the 'Atlantic Coast Express' on summer Saturdays, has lasted ever since.

The 'slam door', thirty second stop Southern Electric, was and is, the most marvellous suburban network in the world that you could possibly imagine at least outside Japan. Over eighty years old now, it still carries millions of London commuters marvellously, uncomfortably, and reasonably reliably most of the time, so that successive governments have flatly refused to invest to improve it, right up to now.

This book is emphatically not about the Southern Electric. Most of my SR journeys were on non electric lines, and were steam hauled over those parts of the route which had the third rail for suburban trains. After forty years of nationalisation, and changing times, most people do not realise that loyalty to the company extended to the passengers. True, many of them knocked the Southern but many more would invariably take the SR to reach the places mentioned in the next chapter, and nothing would induce them to take someone else's service.

When Dr Beeching removed the entire Southern west of Salisbury and Dorchester and handed it to the Western Region, the Salisbury-Exeter portion was soon singled, as 'the proper way' to Exeter is from Paddington. But many people feel differently and Salisbury-Exeter is now part of the Network South East, while Paddington-Exeter is part of Great Western InterCity. Unless there is total upheaval in the commuting way of life, and everything is done by modems and personal computers, and telephonic conferences, I expect Basingstoke-Exeter will finally obtain old fashioned third rail electrification, while Inter-City is already getting overhead wires from Paddington to Reading, although this is primarily intended for Network South East's suburban trains and the proposed link to Heathrow. NSE extends down the Exeter line only to Bedwyn, which for the last seventy years or so, has been the end of the GWR's London Division.

So somewhat naturally, the expert passengers who, unlike me, thank goodness, have had to use it every day, have made themselves heard in no uncertain manner, and may have caused BR to get rid of the name Southern, after all the rest of this book was written. As for knocking the Southern, they have transferred their complaints to Network South East, whose electric trains unlike Southern Railway ones, will not run properly when there are leaves on the lines or, 'the wrong sort of snow' has fallen, though Network South East was created many years after the SR was nationalised to amalgamate, at last, BR's London suburban services. About now the Sector, as NSE is called, will be taking over the whole remaining Southern Region tracks, I understand. What Kings Lynn, Huntingdon, Cambridge, Oxford, Yeovil or Northampton have to do with South East Britain, nobody who puts FRGS after their name is in any position to say. It is true that relaying BR's folly in ripping up the Snow Hill Tunnel tracks under Central London, enables people in Bedford to visit Brighton and Guildford and Orpington without change. More to the point, Thameslink as this service is called, links Luton to Gatwick Airports, something scarcely mentioned in the railway press. This could prove useful for air passengers if Luton ever develops a network of scheduled services.

As for the frightful notion that trains from the Eastern Section should run into the Western Section holy of holies, Waterloo, it has cost £14 million and they are separated off from Western Section trains, all to please HM Customs. Ordinary Eastern Section trains have their own station at Waterloo (East), now separated, but at one time connected by a line running across the pedestrian terminal concourse with no barriers.

Now that perhaps you have caught an inkling of the flavour of the splendid Southern, serving all the very nicest parts of England, certain other things need defining, so that you may better understand the way that it was. The Line, in these pages, means the GW, the one with a Superintendent, when railways like the Southern called such a post the

Traffic Manager, since they started life, like me, in the 1920s, not 1835. 'Southern' means the Southern Railway Company, Limited, until 1948, and BR Southern Region thereafter.

I was privileged to meet several outstanding Southern officers, who unlike the grand GWR, would at least talk to you; among them Sir John Elliot, David Kirby, Robin Sinfield and John Rogers. They knew *all* about the Southern, from Bath (Weston Junction) to St Malo, and Leysdown to Padstow.

But it is high time to stop harping on about The Line, and introduce the reader to Southern metals in the most distinguished way, which set the Southern apart from all the other railways of Britain for forty-four years, World War II excepted. It is five o'clock in the morning. Outside your carriage window, a bright electric light reflects against a white painted steel wall which makes its blaze more dazzling. Should this fail to arouse you, men dropping chains onto steel plating below the window, should do the trick. A refreshing sea breeze comes through this window, which will not open fully, replacing the stuffy night atmosphere. Distantly a shunting engine can be heard, the faint pant of its Westinghouse pump, mingling with the dead slow chuffs from its chimney. Now men are pulling wires underneath your coach, releasing Westinghouse air brakes with that chromatic sigh that has been eliminated by modern air brakes, and is forgotten. A thud, as the special SR brake van, mounted on a long carriage underframe, called a *Queen Mary*, couples onto your coach, which runs over a sort of bridge past an unmistakable British bobby in his distinctive policeman's helmet, and past several official-looking people earning large salaries, apparently by doing nothing. Soon, it stops, and then lurches backwards past a dock with a ship in it, a large signal box, a turntable, and then over an array of complicated cross lines, into an imposing station with overall roof. The shunting engine goes away, and there is a quiet pause.

Presently a pair of those 4-4-0s the Southern was always so fond of, an 'L1' heading a 'D1' take you away in a different direction, and outside the window the sun dances on the English Channel. There is a glimpse of verdant countryside steeped in history, the magic 'something' that fascinates foreign visitors to England, though they can never quite take hold of it, soon lost for the rest of the day as the sun goes in. While the train is in a tunnel, sunshine is replaced by a grey sky surrounding innumerable, rather sad little houses. Unheralded and unsung, you have slipped unobtrusively onto the Southern Railway of England, without, joy of joys, any change of carriage since you went to sleep in it in France, or tiresome walks through inspection halls, or a teeming journey on a one class only ship. For you have disembarked upon the Southern in a Wagons-Lits sleeping car of England's only through international train, created by the Southern, the Nord of France and Wagons-Lits in 1936, the 'Night Ferry'.

Chapter Two

Southern down 'The Line'

When asked which Southern steam engine they think of first, most people instantly reply a Bulleid Pacific. The first Southern engine I think of, is certainly a Pacific, but minus a tender. A Gilbert & Sullivan kind of engine 'Tripping hither, tripping thither' like the fairies in *Iolanthe*.

Why? Because it was the first you saw, when progressing down 'The Line'. What was it doing? Resting, of course, attached to one of those funny Southern brake vans which were so much shorter than the underframes that carried them. No doubt the rest was unintentional, because most probably it was waiting for a signal to cross 'The Line', filled as it was by a seemingly endless procession of 'Kings', 'Castles', 'Halls', 'Stars' and 'Saints', rushing to or from Paddington. So there it was, waiting at Old Oak Common to go tripping back along the West London Railway, to where it belonged, in Feltham Yard.

It seemed to me typically Southern to have an enormous express tank engine to do what the GWR would have done with one of their ubiquitous pannier 0-6-0 tanks. The lowly state of this SR 4-6-2T was marked by the rather hideous Urie short chimney, with no lip. The design was there (first cousin to a 'King Arthur'), the patterns were there. The pony truck would be useful when running backwards, and enabled larger quantities of coal to be carried I believe, than that of their similar hump shunting cousins, also of Feltham Yard, the 4-8-0 tanks, with no pony truck beneath the bunker. The enormous side tanks prevented the Southern from having to buy somebody else's water, when 'foreign' tripping over somebody else's line. GWR pannier tanks were forever at the water column, SR enthusiasts were wont to remark. It must also be said that the engines looked elegant enough when in BR days they arrived at Waterloo at the head of grand trains like the crack 'Atlantic Coast Express' having come all the way from Clapham Carriage Sidings with the empty stock. They were painted green at one time for this duty and for working special trains to Ascot on race days, but were latterly black. These 4-6-2 tanks were not as elegant as the next one you would see as you progressed down 'The Line'. If there was no other SR engine lurking in Acton (GW) yard, this would be one

of Mr Stirling's 4-4-0s with tiny tenders that had outside frames, waiting to leave Reading for Redhill. They had enormous driving wheels,
with a square-ended leading splasher for the very necessary sand,
needed for starting. Much more elegant than the next one, an S11,
another SR 4-4-0 just off the Basingstoke branch train, operated with SR
carriages, which insisted on using the GW shed at Reading, when the
SR had a perfectly good shed of their own there. Grouping or no grouping, a Western Division engine could not possibly go off a GW working
into an Eastern Division shed. After all, LSWR practices were the ones
the SR liked best to employ, though SR engines did eventually use the
SR shed at Reading when overnighting from Basingstoke. This was
because the great Sir Herbert Walker was an LSWR man. As you can
read in the late Charles Klapper's excellent book, he *was* the Southern
Railway.

My progress down 'The Line' usually ended at Newbury where, before
the advent of BR, a Southern engine could only be seen on race days.
After this no more intruders appeared before Exeter St Davids, where
a battery of tank engines, mostly 'E1R' 0-6-2s, but also 'Z' class 0-8-0s
could be found waiting between the Up and Down main lines, ready to
bank any SR trains up the 1 in 37 to Exeter Queen Street, later called
Central to entice traffic from the GWR. Lastly there was Plymouth
North Road, with more 4-4-0s, often the fabulous 'T9s' in later years,
and sometimes 'N' class 2-6-0s, or West Country Pacifics in BR days,
proceeding in the Up direction round the corner to their SR Friary Terminus, giving a good view of Laira shed, rather better than that to be
had from any GWR train.

There was a pause at Plymouth North Road, while the GW engine
was changed for something light enough to traverse Brunel's wonderful Saltash Bridge, leading into Cornwall. The Southern appeared quite
close by at Devonport, where there is a BR connection today and then
it could be seen, far below, skirting the *Tamar* on its way up to London
by way of Tavistock, where once it used the GWR branch to reach
Plymouth.

And at last you were rid of the Southern, unless of course you alighted at gloomy Bodmin Road into the GWR's little branch train with its
cheerful 2-6-2 tank, setting off for Bodmin General, after which the
Southern was encountered again in the form of the Bodmin and
Wadebridge railway which we have already mentioned.

In the West of England, the Railway Bus was a pioneer. GWR buses
at Slough appeared with Cornish number plates, because the Duchy
made no trouble at all about GWR motor buses which had been operating there for over twenty years by the time the Southern was formed.
Matters were different in Devon, and Chagford is forever distinguished by having pre World War I competition between the GWR and
the LSWR when neither had a railway there. The Southern took over the
Exeter to Chagford route which rivalled the shorter GWR one from

Moretonhampstead, where of course the GWR had more than one road motor. The second one was based at the *Manor House Hotel* to convey the GW's hotel guests to and from their trains. At first the LSWR had steam buses. The single Karrier bus on the route was the only one run by the SR. At this time the GWR was running about 200 buses. Devon General took over the route in 1924.

Far more worrying to the LSWR than buses, was the electric tram. Perhaps more than anything else this was what persuaded Sir Herbert Walker to begin the electrification of the LSWR suburban lines around London, in particular where they suffered severely from competition from trams at Wimbledon, Kingston, Hampton Court and Hounslow, because in this area the trams belonged to the Underground Combine instead of wholly to the London County Council and the various local boroughs, who were slow in arranging through running.

Early on the London General began running buses to Windsor, Staines, and worst of all Guildford, and these suburban buses fed traffic into the trams, unlike the GWR's road motor that filched Southern traffic at Ascot for their own railway at Windsor, and was itself in competition with the London General between the Royal Borough and Slough. The LGOC hated competition, it liked shared monopolies, so the two great concerns soon came to an agreement.

Busy with amalgamating the three constituent railways, Sir Herbert Walker does not seem to have bothered about buses until too late, partly because the railways had no powers to run them. Thus even the GWR did not start new routes in the early 1920s though it reinstated ones which they had abandoned in the war, due to shortages of vehicles through requisition.

So my usual recollections of the Southern have mostly been made from somebody else's vehicles, the splendour of a Great Western carriage or the comfort of the top of a bus. Nowadays these great double deckers have all too often disappeared. Whereas the Southern's 'Atlantic Coast Express' stopped on weekdays to detach through coaches here and there, and divided at Exeter Central into Plymouth and Ilfracombe portions, the Great Western's 'Cornish Riviera' slipped coaches without stopping, at Taunton, one of which carried the roofboard 'Paddington, Barnstaple & Ilfracombe'. On Saturdays, the GW like the SR, ran a whole part-train from London to Ilfracombe, and by avoiding the GW terminus at Barnstaple, using the third arm of the triangular junction shortly before the GW's Victoria Road station, the GW engines would continue to Ilfracombe, frequently with an SR pilot or banker, as the line had severe gradients. The weekday single, or pair of carriages would be attached at Barnstaple Junction to an SR train for Ilfracombe. The GW engine, having run round its train at Victoria Road, proceeded, tender first, down onto the Southern.

Just before the end of the 'phoney war', around Easter 1940, a matter of weeks before Hitler started his blitzkrieg on France, leading to the

SR's finest hour, when it carried away in dozens of troop trains, the survivors of Dunkirk, my father packed my mother off on holiday. My mother chose Hartland Quay, North Devon, miles from anywhere, and I was sent too. She would have liked to go to London, but it was considered unsafe.

Thus I travelled along one of the very nicest and prettiest pieces of the Southern main line, from Barnstaple Junction to Bideford, and why it is now shut to passengers I simply cannot imagine. But Barnstaple, gaunt, gloomy, under a rock so it is perpetually in the shade, and open to howling draughts which are funnelled by the rock, was just my idea of an SR place, instead of sunny Southern seaside with 'Sunny South Sam'; remember him?

Our GWR train expired at Barnstaple Junction. Porters (yes, there were still porters) came along, banging the doors, for of course, these were Great Western carriages whose doors did not stay shut unless you turned the handle. So we caught cold on the draughty platform, as the GWR's Mogul speedily set these nice warm coaches back into a siding, and went off to turn (with difficulty on the SR's turntable, as related in *Gone with Regret*).

On the Southern, suburban commuters could not be bothered, unlike GW passengers, to pause to shut the doors in their eagerness to get to work on time. So the staff were faced with endless trains of empty coaches at London termini, all with open doors. To speed this up, the SR invented the slam-door latch. The handle was sprung resting open at forty-five degrees instead of vertical. If you swung the door to close, the latch hit the edge of the jamb, which moved the latch inward in turn releasing the handle which then fell into the horizontal. Nowadays any trains without sliding or plug doors, which can be opened or shut by pressing buttons, are said to have slam doors. There is great agitation about them, as when not fitted correctly, they can appear to be shut but are actually only closed, flying open if you lean against then, with fatal results to passengers. In 1992 somebody wrote to the *Railway Magazine* complaining about this name, and complaining about the noise. It's quite true, in peaceful suburbia, or Barnstaple Junction for that matter, all is quiet, much more so with no steam, until people go along the train, slam, slam, slam, slam, slam. This noise and SR pea whistling disturbed the area. Nowadays people blow whistles much less than they did then.

Presently the Exeter to Ilfracombe train arrived. Its superior coaches came from Waterloo, its Exmouth Junction engine was yet another 'N' class Mogul. The Bideford main line looked uncommonly like a branch; moreover it had single track.

The Ilfracombe train turned sharply right over the single track bridge across the *River Taw*, to Barnstaple Town, where the wicked Southern had ripped up the tourist attraction, in 1935 (The Lynton & Barnstaple narrow gauge railway, if you cannot guess what the attraction was), which, sadly I never saw. That part of North Devon is exceptionally beautiful, in a word, exquisite; but not of course, *Glorious* as the GW described their part of Devon. When most people compare the Southern with the Great Western, they do not compare the respective attitudes of Waterloo towards the Lynton & Barnstaple, scrapped in 1935 and torn up, and Paddington towards the Vale of Rheidol still running today. Had the GWR had a London-minded board, would the Vale of Rheidol still be there today?

Thoroughly chilled by now, the Bideford three coach branch train drew into the platform behind an 'E1R' 0-6-2T of Brighton origins. For me, anything was better than a Drummond machine. Off we went, parallel to the *Taw*, to the coast. The yard at the first stop, Fremington, was full of loaded coal wagons, and they were not just domestic coal wagons, some had 'Loco' on them. There might be a war; there might be requisitioned ships; there might be mines in the Bristol Channel, but not for all the world would SR Welsh loco coal go via the hated GWR. A SR man ran the Railway Executive Committee again, Sir Herbert Walker had had the job in World War One, now it was the turn of Sir Eustace Missenden, General Manager, of the SR from 1939 to 1946. Later in the war, the SR took over the coal trains at Salisbury, for Southampton. I do not think any coal went via Yeovil, except maybe for some local domestic destinations, and nothing was transferred via Chard, except again, local items, as far as I am aware.

So there the little colliers were, steaming into Fremington, as I presume they had for the last forty years, where a grab arrangement loaded the wagons, and an Adams 0395 0-6-0 was shunting them and no doubt hauled away the completed coal train, as traditional an engine as the rest of the astounding scene. But the coal ran on SR metals, all the way from South Wales, which was what mattered. In LSW days it undoubtedly came from colliery to port over some proud Welsh valley independent line (like the 'Taff Vale Railway') that was not GWR until forced to be, at the grouping of the railways in 1923. So not one penny was paid to the rival for loco coal. The colliers were probably cheaper than the rates the GWR would have charged, in any case.

The next stop was at Instow, with more coal wagons in the yard. Soon after this, we started up the estuary of the *River Torridge*, equally as pretty as the *Taw*. Here was Bideford, and an expensive twenty-four mile taxi ride, at least it seemed like twenty-four miles, up and down the steep Devon hills to Hartland Quay. The Southern National 119 service used Tilling-Stevens buses still, with their new style radiator. You had to walk a good mile to Hartland where they started from the Square.

Therefore I was never able to explore on to Torrington and the mysterious 'North Devon and Cornwall Junction Light Railway' which was not completed until 1925, by which time the Southern National's predecessor, the National Omnibus and Transport Company of

Chelmsford, was established in Bideford, Barnstaple and Bude. The Light Railway meandered in search of china clay and the SR's remote Halwill Junction, where the line to Bude diverged from the SR's Exeter-Okehampton-Wadebridge line. I have never been to Halwill, and not even the SR loco coal for Bude and Wadebridge sheds seems to have gone over the ND&CJLR, which despite all those pompous initials usually offered only a mixed train, with one coach and an engine. It made an end-on junction at Torrington Station with the line from Bideford, towards which our 'E1R' departed, after taking water at Bideford. The SR rented the line from the independent Light Railway Company. It was the last line to be built by Colonel H. F. Stephens. (See Chapter Nine).

We came back the same way a week later, but this time all was quiet. There was was no collier at Fremington. That was my first experience of what is usually called the 'Withered Arm'. It went on withering far too long for my money, In the late 1950s I visited Plymouth Friary, before Beeching's plans for the 'Withered Arm', swept to oblivion the lines from Okehampton to Bude and Wadebridge and even part of the ND&CJLR so soon after construction. The passenger service ended at Barnstaple and the line from there to Ilfracombe was torn up too. The Plymouth line was due to close, except for a small piece near Plymouth to Gunnislake, via the GW line through Devonport, and the Exeter-Barnstaple line, but of course he could not get away with it as the line is needed to the SR quarry at Meldon which still supplies most of all BR's ballast from Penzance to Reading and Brighton and all points south west of this line. I only went to get a better look at Laira shed from the carriage, still filled with 'Kings' and 'Castles', the line being GW too, except for thirty-seven chains at the Friary end. In a few minutes we were inside the SR's gloomy, echoing terminus, great, gaunt and sad, slamming doors echoing all round the building. I never saw the 'Atlantic Coast Express' set forth from that gloomy terminus at Friary, I suppose behind a Mogul and later a Bullied West Country 4-6-2 to manage Meldon Viaduct, which had a weight restriction.

In retrospect, when rather than change the engine, BR InterCity takes off the through London trains to Harrogate, Shrewsbury, and now Blackpool or runs diesels to Aberdeen, wastefully under the wires for over 300 miles from London to Edinburgh, the ACE with its nine separate portions, detached along the way, seems wonderfully civilised. Bulleid gave the 'Atlantic Coast Express' nice coaches, I believe, but you do not suppose I ever went in them? Let us recall this civilised train and all its different portions on summer Saturdays, in 1939, instead of a single carriage shunted onto the various branch trains along the way, for those who would not have been seen dead on the 'Cornish Riviera Express'.

The peak working of the 'Atlantic Coast Express' on summer Saturdays in 1939 was:

10.24 am Waterloo - Ilfracombe with Restaurant Car
10.35 am Waterloo - Ilfracombe with Restaurant Car
10.40 am Waterloo - Padstow with Restaurant Car
10.54 am Waterloo - Padstow with Restaurant Car
11.00 am Waterloo - Torrington, Bude & Plymouth with
Restaurant Car to Exeter and separate trains
from Waterloo to Exmouth, Sidmouth, Seaton,
and Lyme Regis but these four did not carry
ACE roofboards.

With hindsight I realise that only World War II prevented the Southern from doing something about its 'frightful' 4-4-0s and its 'odious' 0-4-4 tank engines. They would spend the minimum and electrify as soon as possible. How different to the LMS, who had no engine policy until 1932, borrowing Maunsell's 'Lord Nelson' plans for the 'Royal Scots', and then they simply copied the GWR under Stanier. The Southern was full of quirky initiatives, in backing the ND&CJLR in the first place for instance, as late as 1925, and for building brand new Pacifics in the middle of the war, when only mixed traffic engines were allowed. Bulleid's *Channel Packet* (with SR houseflag on the name-plate) was, do not forget, a mixed traffic engine. The 'Merchant Navies' were not much good on freight trains, of course (nothing is said that I know of, as to whether they hauled the Salisbury-Southampton coal trains), but were supposed to be needed for the troop trains required for D-Day. The Southern, of course, really did not have enough engines for this operation, so Bulleid got his Pacifics.

What a farce. At the end of the war, it was no longer disgusting to go building nice new express passenger 4-6-2s like it was in wartime, when the general idea was that everybody should be as uncomfortable as possible, and as austere, in the faint belief that this in some way helped the war effort. Even cleverer, it seemed to me, was to build slightly smaller 4-6-2s that could cope with the Meldon Viaduct weight restriction, and were therefore all named after resorts served by the Southern in Devon, Cornwall, Dorset and Somerset – the 'West Country' class. I often wondered if it was a GW enthusiast who thought to abbreviate the class name into the acronym used all over Europe except Britain, for the Public Convenience, WC. At any rate, the SR built a whole lot more, but this time called them the 'Battle of Britain' class. These were used on 'Kent Coast Expresses' until the lines were electrified in the 1960s; possibly their tenders were slightly different, possibly not. The Central Section was by this time all electric, at least in theory, and steam engines as required came from the other two. But there was the Oxted Line, the last SR suburban line to be electrified, on which Marsh's 'I3' LBSCR 4-4-2 tank engines still ran, which looked like smaller editions of the tender engines, for which Marsh was famous (See Chapter Eleven), having learnt his trade with Ivatt.

The last 4-4-2T was withdrawn in November 1953, replaced by BR standard 2-6-4T tanks, usually nicknamed 'Hornby Dublo's' after the OO gauge model by that firm, and also by BR standard 2-6-2Ts. The 2-6-2Ts worked Oxted-Uckfield and to Tunbridge Wells West. They came up to Croydon, but not very often to Victoria. These were in turn replaced by DEMU 3 car sets, and these diesels electrics lasted until 1987, when the line was electrified. Lord Beeching chose to live on this line, but who knows if it influenced his stamp upon BR? There was of course the famous occasion when he was stopped at Victoria without his Gold Pass, and the Ticket Inspector insisted that he paid.

The SR was connected to the entrances of Devonport, Portsmouth and Chatham Dockyards, each of which had great Admiralty railway systems, so secret that no ordinary civilians, not employed in the Dockyards, were allowed to know about them. The Portsmouth Dockyard can be found in Chapter Seven. The SR seems to have caught the idea that Docks secrecy was good for security, for Her Majesty's Customs, and for checking pilfering. The mystique to this gave the SR part of its special allure.

Chapter Three

Early Encounters with
the Southern

At the grouping, Parliament left it to the Companies themselves as to how the mechanics of the amalgamation should work. The Railways Act stipulated the boards of the existing Companies should appoint all the Directors of the new Southern Railway with the stipulation that they should not exceed twenty-one in number. The South Eastern Railway had merely formed a joint arrangement with the London Chatham & Dover Railway, each of which were still separate Companies. After some discussion, the twenty-one seats were split; eight to the LSWR, eight to the SE&C, and five to the LBSC. Of the SE&C eight, the SER took five, the same number as the LBSCR, hitherto its competitor, the LC&D being both smaller and with nothing like so many contacts with the LBSCR as the SER, receiving three. The Railways Act became law and effective from 1st January 1923.

Brigadier General Sir Hugh Drummond, Chairman of the LSWR became Chairman of the new Southern Railway. Sir Herbert Walker, after leading all the General Managers of the Railways while effective Chairman of the Railway Executive Committee during World War I, found that his authority was limited to his old stamping ground the LSWR, as General Manager. The Hon Everard Baring, also a Brigadier-General, became deputy Chairman, succeeding Drummond after only nineteen months as the latter died, in August 1924. Then there was Gerald Loder, who had become Chairman of the LBSCR only in 1922. He was devoted to railways and gardening, though a barrister. He became SR Chairman from 1932 until 1934, following Baring's death. Ex-LSWR Directors included Walker's predecessor as LSWR General Manager, Sir Charles Owens, and Robert Holland Martin, SR Chairman in turn from 1934. He died suddenly in office, ten years later.

A formidable Board for any General Manager. But there was also Sir Francis Dent, who had been SE&CR General Manager from 1911 to 1920 and was regarded as a terror, and Frank Dudley Docker from the LBSCR, who was a very influential industrialist and financier. He was Chairman and principal shareholder of the Birmingham Railway Carriage & Wagon Company, while also Chairman of the Metropolitan Amalgamated Carriage & Wagon Company (later better known as Metro

Cammell). Both these firms built many railway coaches, including Pullman cars.

The southern Companies did not wish to be grouped together at all. So, to prevent the accusation of LSWR dominance, as it was by far the largest of the Companies which constituted the new group, the General Managers of all three Companies were retained on the same salary of £7,500 a year, and continued to manage their Sections of the Southern Railway. Sir William Forbes, a fiery independent character was General Manager of the LBSCR. He was the nephew of James Staats Forbes, who had created the LC&DR, in fierce competition with the South Eastern until 1899, when a joint operating committee was formed, creating the SE&CR. Sir Percy Tempest was the General Manager of this, and both these gentlemen dwelt at London Bridge, of course in their respective offices in respective parts of the station, while Walker remained at Waterloo, with no control over the other two sections.

These autocrats were supposed to work together to produce a SR management. Forbes was persuaded to retire in June 1923 with a golden handshake. He had been totally uncooperative. Percy Tempest was also persuaded to go at the end of December, when he received his knighthood. Both were over sixty, sixty-seven and sixty-four respectively, and Sir Percy died within a year, during which he was appointed consultant to the SR. But throughout the SR's company existence at least, many people continued to refer to the sections of the railway by their old names, and the cast iron notice boards remained - LSWR, LB&SCR, SE&CR all including the initials SR, which alone were picked out in white, along with the notice details themselves.

Sir Herbert Walker's grand design was to electrify all the suburban lines of the LSWR, and after 1923, all of the Southern as well. Apart from the managerial difficulties of 1923 when little progress could be made, the delay caused by World War I and the heavy use and minimum maintenance of the rolling stock during it, caused the steam suburban services to be very run down, particularily on the Eastern Section where wartime traffic was perhaps heaviest.

Alfred Raworth, SE&CR electrical engineer was appointed Engineer for new works. He already had planned a scheme for the SE&CR and meanwhile Walker retained Herbert Jones, formerly of the LSWR, as Chief Electrical Engineer for the whole system. So by 1925 the first electrification on the Eastern Section was ready, along with an extension of electrification on of Western Section lines, begun in 1915-16. All manner of other difficulties and obstacles got in the way of this plan, and in the mean time knocking the Southern became popular and everybody had a go.

Sir Herbert Walker had one main fault, he liked to do everything secretly, and suddenly present the travelling public with a completed project. But with the arrival of (Sir) John Elliot, things began to change.

It took about a year to get the press to stop knocking the Southern. The SR bought space in various newspapers, and Sir John wrote articles under such titles as *The Truth about the Southern*. Naming the 'N 15' class 4-6-0 engines after King Arthur and his Round Table Knights, was almost the first of Sir John's acheivements. When he asked permission from R. E. Maunsell, the engineer is said to have replied 'Tell Sir Herbert Walker I have no objection, but it will not make the slightest difference to their performance.' Another of Sir John's later ploys were large notices or posters in the suburban commuter area with 'DOES YOUR WIFE KNOW' in big letters. In clear but relatively smaller print was added 'that she can get a cheap ticket after 10 am.'

I was far too young to know about these upheavals. Though born in London; and though the Southern was essentially a Londoner's line, as mentioned in Chapter One, my encounters with the Southern Railway were mostly with the steam part of it. But I saw much more of the SR in the Home Counties than in the West Country. In those parts the SR was something you saw, but did not go on. The rival GWR was used to visit London. We had a Daimler car, which was such a costly, temperamental conveyance, we also had a second-hand runabout Standard tourer, bought from my father's sister. Already, you see, the Southern was losing its traffic inexorably to road, though there were so few cars in the 1920s, and forty miles an hour in them was pretty frightening when you met a horse and cart round a corner that needed overtaking, whereas trains normally ran at least at fifty, and important ones touched sixty or more.

The Southern Electric was somewhat remote and mysterious, running about on viaducts across all manner of parts of South London, and barely entered my life, being unable to distinguish from the road, which particular line I was looking at. But with the mystery went an excitement, a verve, a gusto for something different, new and better, that was such a contrast to the serene, affectionate, paternal condescension of the other railways, almost entirely all steam operated, though all had a few electric lines, the GW's jointly owned with the Metropolitan.

I have always felt that much of Southern Electric has that sense of the incomprehensible to the outsider, though it was all quite comprehensible to the commuter who knew exactly what headcode his or her train carried, though they were probably as totally ignorant as the rest of us as regards all the other headcodes and the routes they stood for! The never-being-quite-sure atmosphere prevades the Southern to this day. As I write, the Tory Government was finally ordering the Networker in an attempt to bolster their marginal Parlimentary seat at York, where BREL languished without the order. As it turned out, the Tories lost their seat, but at least Network South East got some new trains. Meanwhile north Kent commuters, as in 1924, complained to media pundits in 1992 how unreliable the NSE, ex-SR had become; never quite sure when they would arrive for work, never quite sure if their particular train had been cancelled this morning; true Southern, as every knocker knows!

The third rail system of DC electrification is at the root of the mystique and menace, that characterises the Southern Electric. To touch it is usually lethal, frightening trespassers into a healthy respect for railway property usually not shown by ardent preserved steam enthusiasts, so that for twenty-five years no steam trains have been allowed onto third rail tracks, though this taboo was at last broken in 1992. The third rail would cause chaos every time it freezes, were it not for the SR's all night de-icing trains, keeping it clear. During World War II, arcing dangerously in the blackout, the homely blue flashes given off by the third rail were allegedly a guide to marauding bombers. It was the true symbol of the Southern. Carrying half a million odd people every weekday, the glorious Southern Electric was shown to the public on a special map, the non-electric lines marked less thickly, running off the map, almost apologetically.

I was introduced to it at Oxshott, at the tender age of three, and I was put off by the bare third rail. Notices marked 'Danger, Do Not Touch Conductor Rails' were festooned about the place. From the handy road bridge, you could admire the little olive green trains in safety, and there always seemed to be one, running from London to Guildford or back. I supposed they passed each other near Effingham Junction. A train went by roughly every quarter of an hour, one way or the other, a total contrast to GW branch trains at home, the appearance of which was something of an event. The trains went past, hissing like snakes, or humming like wasps as some people prefer to say, their collector shoes rattling like rings on curtain rails. Then there was the Westinghouse air pump for the air brakes, something completely alien to anyone brought up on steam trains with vacuum brakes.

Nunga-nunga-nunga-nunga-nunga; but how sturdy they were, unimpeded by leaves on the track, plenty of them of course, or by the snow, though I never saw any snow.

You would not recognize the place today. Oxshott was then just a country village, where development was expected. The development when it came, was discreet and tried to preserve the rural atmosphere. At the station, where the trains came and went indifferently, but with varying lengths of train, the staff were very proud of them. Only years later did I notice that the Claygate-Guildford electrification was completed only weeks before I was taken to stay with my grandmother, though modesty prevents me from assuming that the two events were linked in any way.

Far more intriguing than the Southern Electric, with its engine-less trains and frightening third rail, was the London bus that 'wasn't'. London General buses had been my earliest attraction, lacking altogether from my country home, but giving added joy on occasional visits to my father's London flat. 'They do not have such buses in the country' was how they tried to assuage the loud and anguished cries of my howling disappointment; yet now here they were, running in the country every hour past my grandmother's house. From its open top, the passengers peered over the close wooden fence into the garden. Red and roaring, only the words 'East Surrey' in gold on the side, instead of 'General' were different. How much more exciting than any garden games, to watch it go by, to Esher.

My grandmother was rather religious, and there were prayers and hymns on Sunday, when of course the buses ran every half hour, and every minute over thirty, confined to the house for this home service, was one more missed. A service for which my unfortunate aunt, who looked after grandmother, did her best with the wheezing harmonium, Victorian and gloomy. Rather self-determined, my grandmother detested me and adored my sister, who was exactly like her. After her turn, I was asked to choose a hymn. '416', I piped, without a moment's hesitation, causing a sensation. How, the grown-ups wished to know, did I know the number of Granny's favourite hymn? Easy, just look at the number of the bus outside the door. 'Whatever you do', said my mother severely, and my nurse more tenderly, 'do not let Granny find out!'

My aunt, older than my mother, was more practical. She organised a trip to Epsom, which thrilled me to bits, shaking her umbrella at the advancing bus, to make it stop. East Surreys in theory stopped anywhere in the country, but they sailed past fixed stops put up by the General, and as they usually ran only once an hour or so, they must have lost a lot of custom. Sadly it was a pouring wet day and little was to be seen through the steaming, streaming windows of the lower deck, apart from a 65 General at Leatherhead. Somehow we reached Epsom and alighted in the High Street, by the *Marquis of Granby*. No one-way system, few cars, some carts, and buses a rarity. However a General I had never heard of called 181, proclaiming it was bound for Charing Cross, thrilled me by turning round, in the road! Imagine that today!

My father had kept safely out of the way in his London flat. His mother-in-law disapproved of him, anyway. Not to be outdone, he took me to Hampton Court. However we just missed a pirate bus saying it was going to Hampton Court, whereas all the Generals went no further than Teddington. After a long wait, we took a bus to Hammersmith and boarded a tram. I disliked trams, as they gave me sick headaches. My father was very worried as we had wasted so much time. He had never been allowed to take me out alone before. People today have no idea of the well regulated discipline of Victorian households. 1925 it may have been, but the Victorians clung to their traditions, so disrupted by World War I. He himself was never a very forceful person, but he decided the tram was not on for the return trip. So we took the Southern Electric.

On that first journey to Waterloo, I noticed in the train, this entranc-
ing, now famous Hōvis advertisement. Hōvis were very keen that
people pronounced it 'Ho' to ryhme with 'Oh', not 'Hov' to ryhme with
'Of', as most people ignorantly did, so they put an accent on the 'Ō'
and of course the SR letter code had an 'Ō' with a bar on top, that was
a different destination to plain 'O', which meant several places, of
which Orpington from Victoria, sticks in my memory. In fact the original Hovis advertisement was purely a Western Section version and the
letter codes shown were:-

H	Hampton Court	I	Claygate
Ō	Hounslow	S	Shepperton
V	Kingston		

All recollection of Hampton Court station, the branch up to Thames
Ditton, and on to the split junction seems to have been swallowed up
by Hōvis. The brick viaduct on the Down branch line that carries it up
over the main line is one of the first prominent sights leaving Waterloo
on the main line to the west. On the Up side there is the junction of the
Guildford-Oxshott-Surbiton line mentioned above, effected with the
Up Hampton Court, mingling with the convergence of the Up slow.
Then Surbiton, not yet rebuilt, which was later one of the first to show
off the SR's keen taste in pleasant modern architecture, given the
chance. Many trains run non-stop from Surbiton to Waterloo, making
it important for changing to and from the all stations trains. By com-
parison Berrylands is a small affair. New Malden comes next the junction for Kingston. This branch which forms a loop to Richmond where
it joins the Windsor-Waterloo line (at Twickenham some distance
before reaching Richmond) was the first to be electrified by the LSWR,
to compete with the trams. Kingston is the only such place in the
London area, so the appendage '-on-Thames' is often dropped from its
full title. Many people forget that Kingston and Richmond are very old,
Thames-side towns, so long have they been right on the edge of an
expanded London. At Raynes Park, the branch from Epsom joins right
in the station, the Down side having a V shaped two edged platform.
The next station, Wimbledon, signifies to the country provincial like
myself, that London is reached, for the SR branch to Putney East, is
mostly occupied with District Line trains of the Underground group.
These terminate to the left of the Up local, which at this time carried on
to London on the left of the main through lines, but is now carried by
the 1936 flyover to the opposite side of the main lines. The main line is
four-track from Basingstoke to Waterloo. On the left is the staff halt
serving people going to Wimbledon's large car sheds. On this first
journey to Waterloo, the maze of lines after Earlsfield that constitute
Clapham Junction, the largest junction in England, was simply over-
whelming. Shortly before the station, the four tracks from Brighton
to Victoria come parallel on the right. Why there has never been a sensible crossover junction here, I cannot imagine. Victoria is a far handier

terminus than Waterloo, being close to Buckingham Palace and the Houses of Parliament, with Piccadilly and West End, a short distance away, whereas Waterloo is the wrong side of the river. Such an idea would then have been an anathema to the operators, mingling the sacred ex-South Western with the former Brighton lines. Nowadays far more trains stop than in the 1930s as the handiness of changing trains there, well known in Victorian days, has attained new significance now there are Travel Cards and Network Cards enabling passengers to move more freely about the London suburban system. Cross London connections, such as those from Wimbledon to West Croyden via Mitcham; the Wimbledon-Sutton line mentioned elsewhere, and the Wimbledon-Streatham line leading to London Bridge and Holborn Viaduct by Tulse Hill, make an alternative route to the City than via Waterloo.

It always seems to me odd to have put Clapham carriage sidings yard, used by steam trains, or locomotive-hauled stock as it is now called, squeezed in between the lines from Windsor to Waterloo, and the main LSWR line, so that the Windsor Line platforms are an inconveniently long walk over the footbridge connecting them all. In any country other than Britain, a place like this, offering great opportunities for changing trains, would have long ago had travelators and excalators installed. The backwardness due to lack of investment, is simply not understood by politicians and civil servants who between them are mad about roads instead. Replacing every single stairway with an escalator on the Underground, for instance, would speed things up greatly, as would travelators and escalators at Clapham and elsewhere.

Clapham Yard was too small to accommodate the Channel Tunnel trains which are eighteen coaches long, and so at long last the third rail is to be applied to the line, always known as the West London or West London Extension which in company days was jointly owned by SR, GWR and LMS, leading to Kensington Olympia formerly called Addison Road, where there is a short connection to Earls Court, on the Underground's District Line.

In company days this West London connection was a great route for through coal trains, northern railway companies having their own coal depots reached by running over the SR. It has been under used for years. The platform at Olympia used by underground trains which only call when Olympia has an Exhibition, is totally open, so all visitors to Olympia get soaked. Does anyone care? One of the major exhibitions held at Olympia is the World Travel Market. Travel Agents come from all over the world, where stations at least have covered platforms. However don't knock the Southern, as responsibility for the station has lain with the Western Region since nationalisation until now. Naturally the main line platforms are covered partially. For a time the station was used for the Motorail (car carrying trains). The main connection to the GWR which we met at the start of Chapter Two, has now been shut to make way for the Channel Tunnel trains maintenance depot. At present the SR only runs shuttle trains in the rush hours from Clapham Junction to Olympia, and these have to be diesel powered. The connection from this line passes out of sight beneath all the London lines leaving Clapham Junction to reach the eastern side of Clapham Junction's many platforms. In consequence the egress from Clapham Junction towards London is impressive, about fourteen lines of rails leaving the station. The Western Section has eight lines of rails to Waterloo, more beyond Vauxhall, the four track Brighton-Victoria line veres to the right to climb over them while a double track goods line leads to the lower level entrance to Victoria which serves Stewarts Lane Eastern Section loco and carriage depots. The main line out of Victoria is above this on arches. The lot span the Waterloo lines and it is here there is a new curved flyover costing £14 million has been built to bring the Channel Tunnel trains into Waterloo. The *Trans Manche Super Trains* (TMST) are to be marketed under insipid name of *Eurostar*. Queenstown Road comes next, almost under these bridges and then Vauxhall, opened in 1848 when Nine Elms the temporary London terminus closed. This has platforms on all lines once used for ticket collecting. Down below on the right was the smokey den that was Nine Elms engine shed and locomotive works. The works later moved to Eastleigh and the shed was abolished with the end of steam. It is now the central market, moved out of Covent Garden, called I believe, New Covent Garden Market. Although it could be rail connected, of course it is not.

To arrive at Waterloo the lines proceed on a viaduct wide enough for some eight tracks, or more, and this has been further widened to accommodate the TMST whose platforms begin way before where the former LSWR station's platforms start. The viaduct is not even straight, it has an 'S' bend in it, so all trains must arrive slowly and are frequently stopped outside, among the maze of points by which most platforms can be reached.

But to a small child, it was just bewildering, too much to take in. Waterloo is fully described, with all its component parts, in many learned books, and of course it had its lore. The south part, where the suburban trains start was called Cyprus. Until the 1990s there was a wide carriage road adjoining Platform 11 and it was from here that Sir Winston Churchill's funeral train set off, proceeding onto the Western at Reading for burial near Blenheim Palace in the local church. This has been removed and the lines altered to make room for the TMST, which has to be separated from the rest of the station to please the Customs and Police. In years to come people will wonder how the funeral train could have been started from Waterloo. The roadway was also useful for Royal Mail vans, and marching troops, just two great traffics which are no longer seen at Waterloo, in its time the largest terminus in England, and probably in Europe.

The Waterloo and City Railway, opened in 1898, connecting the terminus with Bank Station, on London's Underground, was the LSWR's first electric line, and only the second tube railway in London. 'The Drain' as it is called, has its own maintenance sidings at Waterloo, as it is cut off from the rest of the system, which is at a higher level. Until recently a hoist connected the two. Until 1941 the service was run by single or two car trains, then new stock was obtained, as mentioned in Chapter Thirteen. Whether it will be able to cope with the large numbers of people from Europe, coming to Waterloo to visit the City Banking institutions for the day, as well as the thousands of commuters, remains to be seen. Will computers, modems and fax machines have any effect on reducing the rush hour?

After that 1925 journey to Waterloo, I was determined to seek out this mystery 181 bus again, and persuaded my nurse to take me to Charing Cross: but there was no sign of it. In the interval, the Underground had extended the City and South London line, now the Northern Line, to Morden. The SR were properly upset by the arrival of the Tube, the only Underground line to penetrate South London any great distance, though the East London line, through Brunel senior's Thames Tunnel, reached New Cross and New Cross Gate stations, respectively on the SE&C and LBSC Railways, before 1923.

The SR had powers to build the new Wimbledon and Sutton Railway, which they opened in 1930. It was built to steeper gradients than former lines, since it was always an electric line. The half-mile of 1 in 44 on a sharp curve between Sutton and West Sutton, earned the line the nickname of the 'Wall of Death'. Fortunately Lord Ashfield, Chairman of the London Underground group which included the London General Omnibus Company, disliked competition, preferring agreement with monopolies. He and Sir Herbert Walker agreed the Tube should not extend further, but in the meantime the General had expanded its feeder network of buses from Morden station abstracting a lot of traffic.

Their Charing Cross route to Lower Kingswood (80) and Walton-on-the-Hill (180), was cut back to Morden, but the 181 disappeared. It had run via Banstead to Epsom, and this part of the route was renumbered 164 and also diverted to Morden, already served by the direct bus route 70 from Epsom. After 1931 this was uniquely run jointly with East Surrey at weekends. On weekdays only East Surrey operated between Morden and Dorking, the General working from Clapham Common to Epsom. Both companies thus ran between Morden and Epsom daily.

My father decided the next excursion would be by car, in the country. When my family lived near Sutton Scotney before I was born, my father was wont to travel to London from Micheldever. We drove the few but lovely miles down pretty lanes of copper beech, winding among the Hampshire Downs, and suddenly, by a small wood which is, I think, no longer there, he presented me with eerie and mysterious trains that popped, screeching, out of a tunnel. Many years later I learnt that this was appropriately called Popham Tunnel. Remember, I had never seen a railway tunnel before. The Great Western line has none at all from London all the way to Somerset, and though there was one on the Didcot Newbury and Southampton line at Winchester, I never went on that railway all the way, until about 1938.

A cloud of dense smoke billowed from the tunnel entrance, and the trains frightened me. Moreover they appeared to be almost continuosly emerging from the tunnel, roaring off down hill, the drivers and firemen leaning out to get fresh air, though now and then a few toiled up the grade in the other direction to disappear as mysteriously as the others emerged from it. My father had no notion why there were so many trains, but was of course delighted that an abundance of them appeared magically as promised. Swarms of trains came whooshing out of the tunnel and when fourteen or maybe fifteen had gone by in the space of roughly forty minutes, he decided enough was enough. Even the 'Cornish Riviera', rushing through Newbury on Saturdays, never came to more than about six expresses.

Micheldever Station still has a grand yard and stables, dating from the time when the Salisbury and Exeter horse-coach met the London and Southampton Railway, a coach which of course ran on to Devon, though no longer starting from London in the time honoured fashion. The station is blessed with a quarry containing sidings, formerly used for retired carriages awaiting demolition, but now serving as a petrol depot. The station is famous in history only because the Pullman Car *Rainbow* was destroyed there in 1936, though nobody seems to know why it was there. But everybody knows the chassis, pardon, underframe was used for the Pullman *Phoenix*, built in Brighton's Preston Park works in 1952 and now part of the 'Venice-Simplon-Orient Express'.

But I do not recall any Pullmans back in 1925. Almost every engine was 4-4-0, with a tall chimney. 4-4-0s on the GWR were mostly confined to branch trains. These were gaunter, with the smokebox in a large single cast stretching to the edge of the frame, chimneys sometimes elegant, sometimes harsh and hideous stove-pipes, and nearly all set back a great distance from the front of the bogie which had, what seemed to my young eyes, an enormous front running plate.

We were some distance away, to me they all looked exactly alike. One or two trains came roaring down behind a 4-6-0 which my father said was a 'King Arthur', because, being fairly new and at that time the SR's pride and joy, he had read as much in the papers. But quite likely it was an 'S15' 4-6-0. Some of the 4-4-0s had boilers mounted on a saddle, sticking out in front. These were the famous 'Greyhounds' known as 'T9s', some were 'L11s' with 5ft 7 instead of 6ft wheels. But mostly they were Mr Drummond's other classes which had not got modern chimneys, such as the 'K10s' and 'C8s'. One of these actually stopped at the station. Obviously the local train. I suspect, too, with hindsight, that at least one of Drummond's former 4-2-2-0 rebuilt as a 4-4-0 engine passed, for he dreamed of the days of single drivers and light trains. Not that these were any length, the puny little engines could not manage more than about eight coaches, when the 'Cornishman' as we always called it, usually had fifteen. Drummond built a single driver for himself with a carriage stuck on. Universally known as 'The Bug', it ran 177,000 miles conveying this autocratic, dour, ferocious Scot, to depots far and wide on the LSWR, no doubt terrifying the staff when they saw his personal conveyance appear. At Micheldever we also saw Adams 'X2s' at the end of their lives, pressed into service on something called a Luggage train, comprised of bogie vans looking like carriages without windows. Amidst them all the local pick up goods came gasping out of the choking tunnel, and stabled itself for a while in the sidings, to let a few grand trains with 4-6-0s go by. A shorter train with an 'S11', I now realise was probably a Down Reading-Portsmouth service. For of course there was no question of which was the Up or Down line. You went Up into the tunnel and eventually, my father said, you got to London. Who on earth could all these passengers be? There was no racecourse like Newbury. Most of the engines had great 4-axle tenders, sometimes bogie tenders, for though some were built with water scoops there were no water troughs on the Southern. One of the 22 Paddleboxes 'F13', 'E14', 'G14', 'P14' or 'T14' – take your pick, came prancing by, with roofboards on the coaches which looked less archaic than most of the others, perhaps the 'Bournemouth and Weymouth Express'.

But the rest, pressed into service by the look of them; whistles screeching, the light from an open firebox door momentarily lighting the smoky tunnel end, were of course Ocean Liner boat trains – for far more than just one liner. In those days when planes could not fly at night or more than about 150 miles an hour, the Liners kept the Empire together for Britain, with regular weekly sailings to South Africa, India, Australia, Straits Settlements (now called Malaysia or Singapore) and of course often more than one departure for America, not forgetting South America by Blue Star Line; though for these, many continental people took the 'Sud Express' to Lisbon.

I never saw all those funny 4-4-0s again. When the dreadful day came and I was torn from my home, to be dumped in a pre-preparatory school at Winchester, described later on, it was 1930, and the SR's Chief Mechanical Engineer was not the awesome Drummond nor Urie his LSW successor but R. E. L. Maunsell from Ashford, where he had collected a staff of ex-GW draughtsmen and produced his 2-6-0, 'N' class 2 cylinder, plus some 'NI' 3 cylinder versions so as not to copy the GWR totally.

More Moguls were acquired from Woolwich Arsenal where they were built in an attempt, financed by the Government, to keep wartime munitions workers, employed in peacetime. A batch of these in kit form were also bought by the Great Southern Railway of Ireland, not tobe confused with the one we are dealing with here, but one prone to knocking as well or so it seems. So out went many old crocks, but not all. Some lasted till the 1950s, as the Southern, of course resented having to build steam when it wanted to extend the glorious Southern Electric.

Bus services were springing up everywhere, Thornycrofts starting Venture Limited, to run buses locally in Basingstoke, so as to get their workers more conveniently into their Thorneycroft motor lorry works there. They took over the Basingstoke-Andover piece of the Aldershot and District's long Aldershot-Andover route, very handy for soldiers stationed on Salisbury Plain whose homes were at Aldershot. Finding the road from Whitchurch, where Thorneycrofts bought the petrol station, entirely unoccupied north to Newbury, Venture began a service which was far shorter from our village to Newbury, where it ran specially past the station, than the Winchester to Newbury railway.

The SR at first had no truck with buses, though after 1929, it invested in several existing bus companies. At around the time that Venture began to operate services into Newbury in competition with the erstwhile Didcot, Newbury and Southampton line, the GWR, one of Thorneycroft's best customers, virtually stopped buying their buses. They did not buy any of the new forward drive Thorneycroft buses although at the same time they bought a fleet of Guys and Maudslays of similar size. Whether this was merely a coincidence or GWR pique at the Venture route to Newbury we shall have to wait for Mr Birmingham's history of Venture Limited to see. The Southern never seemed to have any trains at Whitchurch, though the famous 'Atlantic Coast Express' passed this way. Once I saw a train, with one of Drummond's 0-6-0 tanks, something of a rarity themselves, on the railway from Hurstbourne, through Wherwell and Longparish to Fullerton Junction, designed to compete with the southerly part of the line from Didcot to Winchester. The connection to the main line near Whitchurch was shut by the SR in the 1930s.

So for me, the SR remained something slightly mysterious, and unused, so far as suburban electric trains were concerned. On the other hand I never knew steam on the Brighton Line. I also associate Southern Electric with great Pullman breakfasts, as much a part of England as the great actor Lord Olivier, who is forever associated with the Kippers normally offered on this service. Pullmans began in 1875 between London & Brighton.

I travelled frequently myself, mostly after World War II, in the Pullman of a '6-PUL' usually from either Brighton or Hove to Victoria. Third class travel, later second, was still very cheap by 1992 standards. But this belongs to the next Chapter.

Effingham Junction, August 1950. The two carriages nearest the camera were originally built by the LB&SCR for their overhead electrification system and later converted to third rail. The notice on the footbridge's supporting brickwork, has had the SR out of LSWR, picked out in white.

J. H. Price

The concourse at Waterloo. Sir Herbert Walker's offices were on the first floor. The roadway in the foreground, used for Sir Winston Churchill's funeral procession, has now been replaced by extra platforms to cope with the services displaced from the site of the new terminal for Channel

A 'G16' class 4-8-0T No. 495, passing Earley on a freight from Reading to Feltham Yard, in 1923. The loco, though now operated by the new SR, still carries the initials of its former owners the LSWR, on its tanks. *M. W. Earley*

'A "Gilbert & Sullivan" Pacific' 'H16' class 4-6-2T No. 30517 on an RCTS special train at Earley in 1954. *M. W. Earley*

Two views of the SR shed at Reading.

Above, in 1956, No. 30453 *King Arthur* bearing a Salisbury shedplate, is in ex-works condition outside the shed.

Below, a rebuilt Stirling '01' class 0-6-0, A386, was photographed in 1930.
Both M. W. Earley

Much further down 'The Line', 'Z' class 0-8-0T No. 30956 was on banking duties at Exeter Central in September 1962. *J.H. Price*

SR 'King Arthur' class A448 *Sir Tristram* at Exeter Queen Street around 1926. This station was later renamed Exeter Central. *M.W. Earley*

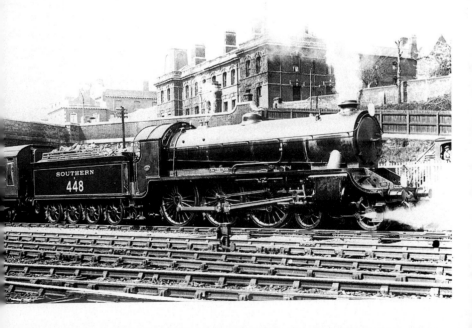

'Merchant Navy' Pacific No. 35005, *Canadian Pacific* on the Down 'Atlantic Coast Express' at Worting Junction in 1949. *M. W. Earley*

A pair of 'M7' 0-4-4Ts Nos 30025 and 30024 at Sidmouth Junction on 2nd September 1962 with the Sidmouth portion of the 'Atlantic Coast Express'. On weekdays the Sidmouth portion of the train consisted of a single coach, on summer Saturdays it was much expanded. *J. H. Price*

Adams '0395' class 0-6-0 No. 0397 at Barnstaple Junction in 1926. Note the square cab spectacle windows *M. W. Earley*

'N' class Mogul 31841 on an Up ballast train from Meldon Quarry, joins the GWR main line from Paddington to Exeter, at Cowley Bridge Junction

Salisbury in LSWR days.

Above: 'T9' class 4-4-0 No. 121 approaches the station.

Below: A pair of 'T9's headed by No. 718 on an express. I always thought that these engines in their original condition as depicted here, looked very Scottish. *Both E. T. Vyse*

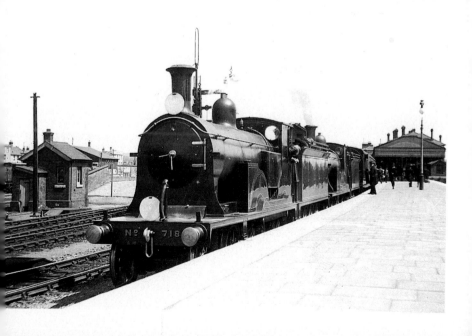

'T9', No. 30718, in its final condition, seen here at Yeovil Pen Mill on 14th August 1960, on an RCTS special. WR Mechanical Horse on left. *J. H. Price*

A few members of Adams' '0415' class 4-4-2Ts survived into BR ownership to work the sharply curved branch from Axminster to Lyme Regis. No. 30584 was photographed at Eastleigh on 14th June 1958, sister engine No. 30583 has been preserved on the Bluebell Railway. Note the square cab windows *J. H. Price*

'S15' 4-6-0 No 30506, now preserved on the Mid Hants Railway, heads a long freight through Basingstoke in 1951. *W. H. Butler Collection*

Though 'T9' 30281 carries its BR number it is still a Southern engine, at least according to its tender, when photographed at Basingstoke in 1951. *W. H. Butler Collection*

The Up 'Devon Belle' near Winchfield on 27th July 1949, showing the Observation Car at the tail of a train of thirteen Pullman Cars. *M. W. Earley*

Waterloo in LSWR days.

Above, **a 'T9', No. 397, leaves on an express.**

Below, **'M7' 0-4-4T No. 21.**
Both W. S. Gray – J. H. Price Collection

Steam days on the Brighton line.

Above: '**D3' 0-4-4T No. 395** *Gatwick,* **at Tooting Bec Common before the First World War.**
C. E. T. Vyse

Below: **The 5.00 pm London Bridge to Brighton 'City Limited' in the 1920s. The engine is former LB&SCR 'L' class 4-6-4 tank, No. 327, renumbered by the SR as B327. These were rebuilt by Maunsell as 4-6-0 tender engines in the 1930s.**
O. J. Morris – courtesy Len's of Sutton

No. 32327, *Trevithick*, pictured elsewhere in its original condition as a 4-6-4 Tank, enters Basingstoke station, in 1951. *W. H. Butler Collection*

The former LB&SCR 'Baltic' tanks were rebuilt as 4-6-0 tender engines. Here No. 32332 *Stroudley* is on shed at Basingstoke, in the company of a Bulleid 'Q1' 0-6-0, in 1951. *W. H. Butler Collection*

Chapter Four

The Brighton Pullmans

The Brighton line was probably the best bit of the railways that were amalgamated to constitute the Southern, though there are many who may think otherwise. The Southern kept their peculiar timetable heads, like London and the South Coast – meaning places on the former London, Brighton and South Coast Railway, and rigidly operated the LBSC as their Central Section. Only in the late 1980s has it been possible to travel by through electric train from London to Southampton via Gatwick Airport, starting from Victoria, which is where most people wish to go to catch trains, rather than Waterloo. When the SR took over, the LBSCR had already started electrifying, the best way, with overhead wires. Sadly, Sir Herbert Walker did not wish to convert his LSWR electrification to overhead wires, for third rail is cheaper to install and overhead maintenance costs were higher than expected.

So the LBSCR was changed over, and, being the shortest distance from the coast, the London-Brighton main line was electrified with the third rail as early as 1932/3. By then there had been Pullman cars and Pullman trains for over half a century. To continue this service was created what were prosaically called '5-BEL' sets of cars. Except that the three sets did not belong to the Southern, but to the Pullman Car Company. They lasted forty years. BR destroyed the service in 1972 and twenty years later, the 'Venice-Simplon-Orient Express' celebrated its tenth anniversary with a special 'Brighton Belle' day.

This is the more remarkable because VSOE said about 1986 when it revived the 'Bournemouth Belle' on Saturdays from Waterloo to Bournemouth (Central), that a 'Brighton Belle' was not viable, since there was no time to serve meals. Fortunately for the 150th anniversary of the opening of the London-Brighton line, the train was chartered to make a series of return trips, serving champagne and canapés only. As a result, VSOE have learnt how to do it.

The 'Bournemouth Belle' has been less successful. Bath and Stonehenge are more popular with the American and Japanese tourists. Whether with privatisation, when organisations other than BR are allowed to run their trains on BR's tracks, the 'Brighton Belle' will return, is hard to say. All the cars have been preserved; two first class kitchen cars *Audrey* and *Vera* are running in the VSOE almost daily. Many others are in various stages of restoration. Brighton is somewhat changed as a destination, though its main attraction, the Royal Pavilion is as enticing as ever, and the comfort of the hotels in their seaside setting, combined with the nearness to all the pleasures of London, deserves a better rail service than is now provided. Brighton Station, built in 1840 by David Mocatta, a pupil of Sir John Sloane, is now a listed building and cannot be rebuilt.

It is, at the moment of writing, ridiculous that BR cannot run nonstop from Brighton to Victoria, as was the case for years, in just an hour's travelling time. The present trains take fifty-five minutes but make one stop as well, the public prefer non-stop trains. And it is equally ridiculous that there are no fast, comfortable non-stop trains between Brighton and Gatwick Airport. That is what makes the study of railways so exciting. You can never be quite sure of the service. Sadly, most people just want service. How it is arrived at, why its quality is not as expected, seems nowadays not to interest the customers, who do not expect as much as previous generations did, perhaps. But then, equally ridiculous to the Brighton line *service* is the total inability to build a high-speed line from London to the Channel Tunnel, until years after it opens.

These gloomy thoughts never entered one's head in the 1930s. Brighton in those days was a veritable Mecca for transport enthusiasts, with a choice of trams, genuine London buses provided by Thomas Tilling, identical to those on the South East London services that stretched to the heart of the City and West End; and a plethora of country bus services run from Pool Valley, by Southdown, perhaps the best company in Britain at the time. There were coach services and excursions galore, and, happily still there, unlike the network of Corporation Tramways, *Volk's Electric Railway*.

Placidly plodding from the Aquarium to Black Rock since around 1883, Britain's first electric railway is the perfect relaxation, especially the toast rack cars in which passengers can drink in the sea air. It narrowly won the race to be Britain's first electric railway, beating the Giant's Causeway Tramway in Ulster by a few weeks. Beyond the depot, Paston Place, the line was on a kind of wooden viaduct above the waves but most of the way it is now on a concrete foundation, on the shingle of the shore. The stolid continuance, the peaceful pace, gives time to half-believe the trams, the trolleybuses, the London buses and the Pullmans if not likely to return, will be replaced by something equally comfortable and convenient.

Ninety-seven years of Pullmans is a long time. Four times longer than the existence of the Southern as a company and twice as long as BR. Almost no trains lasted that long, and in World War I, Pullmans to Brighton expanded into Third (now Second or Standard) class, instead of closing down. Even in World War II, only a direct hit at Victoria put the 'Brighton Belle' in mothballs for the rest of the war.

Air conditioning, piped music and loudspeaker announcements welcoming you on board are all very welcome but do not quite capture the elegance of 'pan-fried' eggs, as though you expected the engine's fireman to fry them on his shovel in the firebox, which the steam engine crews often did, and still do, on some preserved railways. Do you remember 'curled butter?' I have a gadget that does it, somewhere, making the dish far more elegant than today's little wrapped portions – which use more butter, anyway! For me the London to Brighton line is inseparable from gorgeous sardine sandwiches called *Toasted Sandwiches*, of glasses of cider because it was cheap, make-believe champagne, golden crutons in the soup and lovely preserves, no such thing as jam. Then of course *Minute Steak* which always baffled me as the 'Belle' shot through East Croydon non-stop – as no Brighton-bound train does now. Did it mean that they had grilled it in a minute, or was it the size of the thing that was being driven at, for certainly they were small enough? They were four ounce strips of Sirloin steak, cooked one minute on each side, in theory. The name came from the famous *Savoy Grill*, in London, in the 1930s.

Of course there were other things as well besides the heavy brass table light, the double brass racks, the smaller, lower one for the rolled umbrella and the hook on the end for the bowler hat that everybody who was anybody wore in London. There were trains to look at, some with Marsh tank engines, mini versions of the gorgeous 4-4-2 tender engines, that adorned the Newhaven boat train until nationalisation and beyond, superseded by electro-diesels until third rail electrification in 1969 of the Newhaven Harbour Dock lines, when people were forced to use commuter-style sets to reach the Cross Channel ferries. Passing through Purley, the large shed located between the Down Redhill line and the Caterham branch formerly housed the SR's *Royal Train* which was made up of Saloon Brake 7914, Saloons 7918, 7920, Royal Saloon 7930 and Saloon Brake 7919, there was also Royal Saloon 7931, a former SE&CR vehicle fifty-eight feet in length and mounted on six-wheel bogies which was kept at Calais for continental journeys until 1928. In the thirties Royal trains on the Southern were normally formed of Pullman Cars, or if night travel was involved, the LMS *Royal Train* was used.

Then the countryside. Diving through the North Downs on the Redhill avoiding line, called the Quarry Line, by which the LBSCR finally escaped sharing the South Eastern track and their Redhill delays, where their line parted as we will see in Chapter Nine. Dreams of exotic destinations as the 'Belle' shot past the end of Gatwick Airport through the station in full view of the travellers waiting to be called to their planes. Then Balcombe tunnel and on through glorious Sussex, and the superb viaduct over the *Ouse* with its unspoilt view of the farms below. Bungalows, housing estates, ever growing at Hassocks, after the older dormitary town of Haywards Heath and the nearby junction at Keymer where lesser Eastbourne trains must wait for the 'Belle's' passage. Finally Clayton tunnel through the great South Downs which keep the frost away (very largely) from the coast and Brighton. Past Preston Park Pullman works, established 1928, and Preston Park itself, municipally magnificent as though waiting for plaudits from the late Sir John Betjeman and then an arrow pointing with 'Brighton' above on a huge green board, perhaps copied directly from the French approach to Paris. One of Mr Stroudley's little Terrier 0-6-0 tanks could be seen waiting to take the goods to Kemp Town, or maybe go shunting at Newhaven, crossing the *Ouse* on the main road bridge there among the traffic. And above all, the Southern Electric *Squwark*, straight out of the *Dance of the Hours* ballet music, incidentally used at one time by Italian light railways, too. Somehow the standard two tone horn copied from GW railcars that got it from the French, seems tame, though BR obviously finds it safer.

Above all the disinfectant in the lavatories or the air freshener, identical with those used by Wagons-Lits everywhere, which more than anything reminded one of the association between the two companies. This tie-up has never been explained properly, and nowadays dry history does not get revealed unless it is slipped in as part of the service. George M. Pullman got his cars onto the Brighton line in 1875, starting the first all-Pullman service on the line in 1881. After his death Lord Dalziel of Wooler, Davidson Dalziel as he then was, bought Pullman's British assets in 1907, giving Wagons-Lits the right to the name on railway cars in all the rest of Europe and Egypt, including Channel Tunnel trains when the Tunnel should be built. What foresight, to provide for this, eighty years before it happened!

In the middle of World War I, the Mitropa Company was formed in Germany with the intention of requisitioning all Wagons-Lits cars in Germany, and making new contracts to run these throughout Central Europe and also Denmark. Hence the title Mitropa (Mitteleuropa shortened). Having usurped everything, the Pullman name would be usurped as well on saloon cars, Dalziel thought.

So he formed the Pullman Car Company Limited (which is still in existence) which had a substantial Wagons-Lits holding, though not a controlling interest. The Company was quoted on the London Stock Exchange, it had independent shareholders but Dalziel was by far the largest, and was elected Chairman for life. Immediately he set about registering the name Pullman in neutral Denmark, as belonging to Wagons-Lits. At the end of the war, Dalziel was very eager to get Pullmans up and running in Europe, to attract the American tourist market. George Pullman had previously only established himself in Italy, and in a very small manner, with less than a dozen cars.

René Nagelmackers, son of the founder of Wagons-Lits, Georges, who died in 1905, had married Dalziel's daughter. Lord Dalziel had become Chairman of the Executive Committee though not President of the Company, this position being held by a Frenchman, Monsieur Despret. At this moment the French Government, fearful of further bad railway accidents after so great a loss of life in the war, decreed that all new express rolling stock should be steel, to prevent the awful fires when gas ignited in wooden bodied coaches, very often, following an accident, which usually caused wooden bodied coaches to telescope.

The only firm that could rapidly produce all-steel coaches was Leeds Forge, who had built all-steel gunpowder vans during the war. They produced forty new sleepers, the first to be blue and gold, for the Calais and Paris Mediterranean Expresses, promptly dubbed the *Blue Train*, Wagons-Lits' other stock being varnished teak.

The French faction now wanted steel dining cars, while Dalziel wanted Pullmans to spread over Europe. New wooden cars were accepted in France only if they were running in from another country. Firms like De Dietrich in France and the Birmingham Railway Carriage and Wagon Company in Britain, were tooling up to make all-steel coaches like Leeds Forge but none were ready until 1925-6. So Dalziel took ten Pullman Car Company Pullmans, ordered in 1924 and delivered early 1925, and sent these to Italy to run into France along the Riviera, from Milan to Cannes. A Pullman Car Company conductor went with the cars, to train the Wagons-Lits' staff.

By 1925/6 Wagons-Lits had obtained new all-steel saloons for the French portion of the 'Paris-Madrid-Lisbon Sud Express' (owing to the wider Spanish gauge passengers had to change to sleeping cars at the frontier). These saloons mostly had compartments or coupés, but one half of the car was an open, Pullman-style saloon, each car being called *Voiture-Salon-Pullmann*. Some of them had kitchens, in Pullman tradition.

In 1926 Dalziel made another agreement with the Wagons-Lits Executive Committee under which the Pullman Car Company would build and furnish steel Pullman cars for Wagons-Lits to buy and operate on services to be mutually agreed, of which the first was the Paris-Calais 'Fleche d'Or', celebrating the Golden Jubilee of Wagons-Lits in 1926. The profits from these cars would be shared fifty/fifty, after Wagons-Lits had deducted their operating costs, but this would not apply to cars already ordered or bought by Wagons-Lits, such as the Sud Express cars just mentioned above. The new Pullman Cars, which were subject to the agreement, would be numbered in the 4000 series for easy identification by the accountants. The Pullman Car Company would seek out the services and invite Wagons-Lits to run them, but should Wagons-Lits decline to do so, then the Pullman Car Company itself should have the right to provide and run Pullmans on these services themselves.

The existence of this agreement was never discovered before 1989, and it was of course a relatively simple matter for the Chairman of the

Pullman Car Company to get the Chairman of the Executive Committee of Wagons-Lits to sign it, for they were one and the same person, Lord Dalziel himself, who had thought it up. Unfortunately he died, early in 1928. But before he died, it seems that Wagons-Lits were unwilling to buy and run English-built steel Pullman cars on the Andalusian Railway in Spain. So the Pullman Car Company supplied them to the Railway and undertook to staff them, for the first year. Built by Metropolitan Carriage Wagon and Finance Company. in Birmingham, they look virtually identical to those supplied for the 'Golden Arrow (Fléche d'Or)' and other Pullman trains run by Wagons-Lits under this agreement. As Wagons-Lits had staff, and supply depots in Spain, and the Pullman Car Company had none of these, Dalziel arranged for Wagons-Lits to staff and supply the cars for a year on behalf of the Pullman Car Company, when they started running. A similar arrangement was made with the Vascongados narrow gauge railway in Northern Spain (San Sebastian-Bilbao), whose Leeds Forge built steel Pullmans were also staffed for a year by Wagons-Lits. Some of these cars are now running, re-furbished, in the 'Trans-Cantabrico' luxury cruise train of the FEVE.

This was why the Pullman monthly publication, the *Golden Way*, distributed in bookstalls and on the cars in certain cases, containing all the trains in Britain that had any Pullman Car service, began with 'Continental Services' as though they belonged to, and were operated by the Company. At this time, the British and American public had to be persuaded that 'abroad', as they called it, they would be assured of the same high standard of Pullman service. As the cars, with the exception of the 'Fléche d'Or' service, which used the same upholstery and cutlery as the Pullman Car Company (with a different crest on the cutlery) appeared to their users to have nothing whatever to do with the Pullman Car Company, this was very puzzling. The English Pullmans, except for two sent on to Egypt, returned to Britain in 1928. One of them, *Ibis* runs in the 'Venice-Simplon-Orient Express' Pullman train, though as it is now sixty-eight years old, it is now the reserve car.

There was great concern that Lord Dalziel's large personal holding in Wagons-Lits and in the Pullman Car Company, would be subject to very high death duty in the UK. This was circumvented by the establishment of the International Sleeping Car Share Trust, said to have been successfully completed just one week before Lord Dalziel died. As a result of these arrangements, Wagons-Lits had a controlling interest in the Pullman Car Company, though it was not a subsidiary. A lawsuit ensued over the agreement, since it said nothing about the fifty/fifty sharing of any loss!

There is a photograph of the 'Fléche d'Or' whose four Pullmans include a pair of 'Sud Express' ones, although Wagons-Lits was not supposed to use these on services run under the agreement. In Spain for service on the Norte and MZA railways, Wagons-Lits obtained the last teak Pullman cars of the Company, and supplied the meals from their adjoining dining car. These were built in Spain.

Meanwhile in Britain, all-steel composite Pullmans were supplied for the ordinary SR trains to be used in the new Brighton electrification, as well as for the 'Brighton Belle', in 1932. Four years earlier, all-steel Pullmans had been built for the 'Queen of Scots', Pullman (London Kings Cross-Leeds-Harrogate-Ripon-Northallerton-Newcastle-Edinburgh-Glasgow Queen Street) for the LNER, and also five first class all steel cars for the GWR Ocean Liner contract. When the GWR refused to renew this, these cars came to the Southern and were used on the Southampton Docks Ocean Liner boat trains.

But owing to the losses, the Pullman Car Company could no longer afford to supply new composite Pullman cars for the electric trains needed for the 1935 Eastbourne and Littlehampton electrification. The Southern built cars with a pantry instead, which Pullman staff operated to supply passengers at their seats, as had been done from the Pullmans in the '6-PUL' Brighton sets. Thus the well known formation of a '6-PUL' plus a '6-PAN' set making up the main line fast electric trains came about on both the London-Brighton, and London-Eastbourne-Hastings, and London-Worthing-Littlehampton routes.

The Southern Railway was the anchor, virtually, of the Pullman Car Company's well being, as the thirty year contract lasted until 1962 and included the staffing of various SR catering cars such as the Bognor buffets and Eastbourne line pantries which replaced old Pullmans used in the steam-hauled trains. First the GWR would not renew its trial contract for the Torquay Pullman in 1930. Then the LMS refused to renew the Scottish Pullman Restaurant Car contract in 1933, buying up the cars, some of which were only a few years old and continued to run in BR service until the 1950s. Then in 1936 the Great Southern declined to renew their contract on the four third class Pullmans they had been using since 1926. There is a rare colour illustration of one of these unique 5ft 3in gauge Pullmans on page 94 of Tom Ferris' excellent book *Irish Railways in Colour*. In the meantime the LNER had introduced the Supplementary Fare Silver Jubilee in 1935, followed by the luxury 'Coronation', without offering their operation to Pullman. The Pullmans on the Metropolitan Line were built in 1910, and following nationalisation of the Metropolitan Railway in 1933, London Transport gave notice that it would not be renewing the contract in 1940.

When I set about writing *Pullman in Europe* in 1959, I discovered about the bomb at Victoria Station which damaged one of the 'Brighton Belle' sets in 1940. The train later went out of service from May 1942 to the end of the war. I also found that another 1944 bomb which had destroyed all the records in the Pullman Car Company's office, had caused Mr Morris, the Secretary in London, to be using a different list of Car Schedule numbers to that used by Mr Johnson, the Engineer at Preston Park! As you may imagine, I was not the most popular of travel writers around, and all and sundry failed to disclose to me that with the ending of the SR contract and LNER contract in 1962, a major upheaval would overtake the Company. They did tell me that as in 1954 BR had given notice that these would not be renewed, Wagons-Lits had sold its majority holding in the Company to BR. The renewal of their own contract for the 'Night Ferry' for fifteen years from 1960 was possibly due to the seats on their Board for Lord Robertson and Sir John Elliot in 1955. If they had only done this earlier. Who knows, the 'Brighton Belle' might still have been with us a bit longer than 1972.

When these details came to light about 1989, the Wagons-Lits archives also yielded up a Pullman Car list, made fifty years earlier when their engineer M. Pillepich came to Britain to review the situation as explained by an independent report, prepared on request of the Pullman Car Company Chairman, Sir Follett Holt, by a London Transport engineer. M. Pillepich is well known for his 1955 design of stainless steel Budd patent sleepers Type 'P' (named after him) which are now being modernised (They are now called AB30, 10 airconditioned high roof cabins with 1, 2, or 3 berths, leased until 2007 to the Australian, Belgian and Dutch railways by Wagons-Lits). It was a great relief that the only pre-war car list in existence corresponded correctly with the information set out in *Pullman in Europe*!

The Brighton Line Electrics all belong to the 1930s. The line was electrified in such a way, that service began for the public, on 1st January. 1933, after trials and staff training, making it easy for chroniclers to be caught napping by giving 1932 as the year in which services commenced, since all the first SR main line electric sets were built then. The Brighton electrification was a complete breakthrough, in modernisation and frequency of service, but without any decline in comfort.

While the 'Brighton Belle' and the '6-PUL' sets brought some glamour to Victoria, the London terminus of most Brighton line trains, there were some sets, which had a higher proportion of first class accomodation and were designated '6-CIT'. These ran in the rush hours to and from London Bridge from whence many of their patrons went to the Stock Exchange where they worked. Before 'Big Bang' altered everything in the 1980s, in those days the Stock Exchange opened for business at the leisurely time of 10 am.

No reminiscences about Brighton would be complete without a mention of the superiority of Brighton engines over those built by the LSWR. We have already seen how Maunsell, the former South Eastern and Chatham's engineer, improved upon the LBSCR 'E1' 0-6-0 Tanks by giving them a pony truck at the rear and larger bunkers, to make them suitable for the Southern in the far west, beyond Exeter. Here the oldest engines were to be found, Beattie's 2-4-0 Well Tanks. These excellent engines quietly went on operating the Wenford Bridge branch, near Bodmin, for china clay, throughout the whole period of the SR's existence as a Company and well into BR days.

Brighton Loco works built the 0-8-0T Z class. The works were closed in the slump of the 1930s only to be re-opened during the war. After the war they turned out Mr Riddles' Standard BR Class '4' 2-6-4 Tank engines, based on the successful Stanier design of the same wheel arrangement. BR's greatest folly was to go on building a host of newly-designed standard engines, when railways abroad were rapidly electrifying their lines. In this way they simply added to the thousands of different spare parts, needed for the hundreds of steam engines already functioning. The Riddles of British Railways as I refer to them – you will not find a single one in all the 139 pictures in *Gone With Regret*, – were simply not as good as the designs of C. B. Collett. Even though comparable standard locos were on the drawing board, the Western Region was allowed to build a further batch of 'Manors' to Collett's design in 1950.

Other Regions were also allowed to build engines that had already been started. So Brighton works set about building Bulleid's 'Leader' Class 0-6-0 + 0-6-0, the coupled wheels being on two bogies. Bulleid had demanded to build twenty-five of them, untried, from the SR Board of Directors, in 1946. No doubt he wished to get them under way, during that final two years of company activity, before nationalisation. However, Bulleid was such a pro-steam man, and such an eccentric, that after nine years in office, he had to fight hard for his whims to be met. He got authority for five engines, and great secrecy surrounded them because they were not allowed to be built until the prototype was completed and tested. They were called 'Leader' as they were supposed to be way out in front of steam design, and because the driver was positioned at the leading end of the engine, like a diesel or electric one. The idea was to house a conventional engine plus tender size bunker and water tank in a casing with a side corridor with curved sliding doors to the compartment for the fireman. This was connected to both driving compartments. There was a sliding side window on each side of the fireman's compartment, also an inward opening door. When open, I believe these prevented the fireman from being able to get at the coal supply, so it had to be shut when travelling. The heat inside this compartment was intense, and quite unbearable when running chimney first. So the engine needed turning at the end of each test run, when the whole idea was to cut out turning. Externally the engine looked like a diesel perched high above the wheels, to allow access to the wheels and permit them to articulate. Panelling covered the exterior of the wheels themselves, with a large gap below the engine casing, which extended downwards, slightly, between the bogies.

The engine was a total fiasco and was scrapped by the Railway Executive, as BR was then called. Southern Region officers named it the *Bleeder*, according to the late Sir John Elliot. As the boiler and the coal were offset to accommodate the corridor, the engine was heavier on one side than the other, and pig iron had to be placed in the corridor to balance this. It is unclear why there was a corridor. The engine was roughly half as efficient as a 'U' class 2-6-0, and had a huge appetite for coal and water compared to the 2-6-0's consumption. So £276,000 was written off, equivalent I would say of £2 million at today's prices. Bulleid departed to Ireland, where he built another 'Leader' arranged to burn turf, which was another fiasco, apparently. However, don't knock the Southern, BR spent many millions on the *Advance Passenger Train*, of which they were so ashamed they scrapped its comfortable coaches, instead of modifying them for other work.

In 1929, before the Brighton Line was electrified, and before, long before, I ever went on it regularly, an event occured that influenced my life completely. I was taken for the first time to Victoria and to that most romantic of starting points, never used by the 'Brighton Belle' – Platform 2, and was first introduced to Pullmans. It was explained they were not SR coaches. They were painted umber and cream and being colour blind, it seemed to me most appropriate colours for such luxurious, comfortable coaches, since they were so like the Great Western colours. The Southern called itself the *Key to the Continent*, the actual key being the 'Golden Arrow', while Victoria was advertised as the *Gateway to the Continent*. And its just the same today. Every Thursday and some Sundays at 11 am precisely, the Pullman train of the 'Venice-Simplon-Orient Express' sets out for the Channel port in the time honoured way while on the other side of the Channel the sleeping cars that once belonged to the Wagons-Lits Company, wait to take you on to Paris. It is slightly grander than the original and there are no supplements or meal charges because the British and Americans never liked these very much. The revival of luxury rail travel enables something of the excitement and the glamour of the great international trains of yesterday, to be experienced by today's traveller.

Chapter Five

'Victoria 4.30'
Continental Express

'Victoria Station, Chatham side', with these imperious words my father directed the taxi outside 127 Wigmore Street that took us from the London flat and the affection of my nurse, from whom I was parted for the first time in my life, to embark upon the Southern Railway.

Why 'embark?' You might just as well ask, as I did: 'Why Chatham side?' My father explained, how, before I was born there was not any Southern Railway, but two stations at Victoria, side by side. Only long years afterwards did I learn the complicated history of Victoria. I already had sufficient to go on. The Southern was not what it said it was! Had I not seen that formidable old locomotive, with London and South Western Railway on it, plodding up to Newbury with racegoers, three or four years earlier?

'You could, if you like say Continental side' my father added and here was another anomaly. For of course you didn't go to the Continental side, but the Brighton side for the 'Continental Express' to Newhaven. That was Southern lore all over!

Victoria Station was a splendid place. It had a bus station outside, full of London buses leaving for all manner of country places like Potters Bar, or Abridge, or Loughton, and later even Borehamwood. Of course you have to stretch the imagination a bit to call some of these country, but they were outside the London area 1930s speed limit, and Paddington had nothing like this.

The Chatham side, down an alley called Hudson's Place, is of course the 'Gateway to the Continent'. This was a Southern idea, removing all the boat trains from Charing Cross. That you couldn't go by ordinary train to Folkestone from Victoria but only Charing Cross was another astonishing discovery, made years later. Here we are, steeped in Southern mystique. I never hoped to understand it. It was quite confusing enough already. To start with, there was a little board marked 'Calais', though the train did not go there; it only did its best to do so, as I noticed later on. Then the carriage, magnificent in gold and umber and cream paint, was not a Southern one at all. It was a Pullman.

At the back of the train was a sturdy 0-4-4 'H' class tank engine built by Mr Wainwright for the SE&CR. What elegant cab roofs they had compared to those elsewhere on the Southern. It hissed loudly. Donkey engines at Paddington sat sedately and quietly at the end of trains.

Everything was about as different as it could possibly be, from any train I'd ever been in before. Inside the carriage was a saloon with just two compartments at each end called coupés. Even the end doors opened inwards when I had been used to outwards. The massive brass table lamp with its crinkley orange silk shade, shared the table with a bowl of wrapped sugar lumps, with an elegant frieze round the top.

An attendant looked in and asked if we would like tea. Then there was that whistle blowing rigmarole. Not just one whistle, and one guard, but two or three men whose stiffer hats contrasted with those of the great numbers of porters with their cheap looking metal badges, and squashy peaked headgear who had carted off the registered baggage past some Naval looking men, and seized our holdall and little cases and spread them liberally along the racks, among the umbrellas.

How loud and brash it was. All those men making a whoopee noise with their pea whistles, engines whistling in return, and then the most almighty thumps and bangs, shaking the sugar bowl on its spotless white table cloth, making the woodwork of this lavishly ornamented coupé creak, while above all the din the 'chuff-chuff-chuff-chuff-chuff' of the tank engine, its wheels spinning round wildly, introduced me to what I always think of as a typical Southern steam start. No wonder the poor carriage shook like a crazy thing.

Then the bumps and groans subsided, as the Pullman sedately clunked over the railjoints and rumbled luxuriously over the *Thames* at that ten miles an hour which is the speed for enjoying Pullman departures or arrivals. London, as sedate as the Pullman or the *Thames*! Then the train plunged into a network of lines among the slums (though you should not call them slums) in a chaos of expensive bridges and viaducts and embankments, carrying lines above each other, punctuated with the whine of electric three-coach trains, and plumes of smoke from spare steam engines. Palls of smoke fell against the besmirched windows as we ran high above the buses and trams over main roads at Brixton and Herne Hill, then up the long climb through West Dulwich and past Dulwich College into Penge tunnel. Frequent shrieks from the whistle punctuated the cacaphony of rattling tea cups, the sudden roar as the door of the coupé shot open, revealing the attendant and his long silverine serving dish, covered with a cloth, on which reposed toasted tea cakes.

Penge! I thought of my poor nurse, dragged against her will to Bromley on a bus (she was kind enough to arrange to take me there, without any notion how far it was!). How thrilled I had been by the buses marked 'Penge', almost the first time I had ever seen a General single-decker.

How civilized it was. The Southern lumbered along, sedately at thirty miles an hour, past the posteriors of little houses, some with gardens, some without, occasionally crossing a bustling main road on a bridge, then coming to a forlorn looking junction, slowed by signals so that one could read the names: Beckenham, and then Shortlands.

The train roared through a station and my father remarked it was Bromley South. Curious how the bus names and the train names never seemed to match, like the station at West Dulwich – when all the buses seemed to go to East Dulwich, and Bromley North Station, was so much more interesting, bus-wise, than Bromley South. Then quite suddenly, the countryside started.

More chaotic junctions, hidden by trees this time, and good gracious, is this a single line? No, merely one of the Southern's many fly overs and spurs at Bickley, joining the old LCDR to the former rival SER (it has just been remodelled for Channel Tunnel trains). Then Orpington, and the end of the electric trains, with O on the front because they went there. Down into great eerie chalk cuttings, that's the Southern for you, diving mysteriously into weird chalk covered tunnels like Polhill, with sad signal boxes at their entrances. The whole seems to have a vast spell about it, as though the rickety steps, the green tin boards with the white lettering, white as the chalk itself, the brickwork of the tunnels, were all a great part of Britain's heritage. After Polhill Tunnel, the only visible sign of industry was the oast-houses, used to dry hops for beer making. Somehow the boards, and the engines and ordinary carriages too, could never really be anything other than green, bringing to mind Blake's description of 'England's green and pleasant land'. (It is not any more – and the coaches are blue). He also wrote about 'Dark satanic mills', well, everyone knew where they were, down the unmentionable LMS. Oh! no, knock the Southern if you will, recalling what an eternity the train seemed to take to get from London to Tonbridge, where between 1933 and 1970, if you got out at that station you would see 'London Transport' written on some of the buses in the yard, just like at Victoria, though they were painted green, instead of red.

Then after Tonbridge, the long straight haul through the garden of England, the splendid Weald with its orchards and sleepy villages and no main roads at all. Marden, Headcorn and Pluckley came and went, like the junctions at Tonbridge, unnoticed on that exciting day, tucking into the Pullman strawberry jam sandwiches and the ancient Pullman *Quality cake* that always tasted as though it had to make six journeys to the coast and back before it was mature and fit for eating. 'Fruit cake sir?' What an air of elegance they had, these splendid Pullman attendants, waving the dish in motion with the train which suddenly, realizing that at this rate it would never get to the coast at all, began to tear along at sixty miles an hour. What a brave sight, the two (expensive) engines, one behind the other, for no apparent reason save that this was Southern practice. Who was to know that all the brick arched bridges were so flimsy that heavier engines found elsewhere along the Southern could not pass over them in safety?

Past that curious orangery pavillion, built on some hill and subsequently stricken by fire, past Ashford where there was a brief glimpse
of industry as the train flashed passed the locomotive works. So down
to Westenhanger, peaceful and serene. Into a tunnel and out past
Shorncliffe Camp. There is no camp today and as to its serenity this has
been lost to the activities engendered by the Channel Tunnel.

Then came the man, writing out the *check*, last symbol of the once-
American ownership of the Pullman Car Company, as the train swept
round the curved viaduct high over Folkestone and faces peered forth
from the windows at the waves. More whistles as the train dived into
yet more tunnels, running beside the sea, and as usual, surrounded by
chalk. People seeing the seashore began putting on their overcoats and
mackintoshes in readiness for the early evening sailing. The windows
on the right looked across the Up line, to the shore, clear of all smoke
as the engines freewheeled on the last stage of their non stop run.

Slowly they picked their way over Archcliff Junction outside Dover,
past the engine shed and some sidings, separated from the shore by
just a wire fence. The Pullman, once more sedate, clumped over the
crossings, the noise uneven, the flanges squealing against the check
rails, for such was Dover Marine before it was remodelled.

So to rest in another great cavernous station, with wide platforms,
replete with bookstalls, refreshment rooms and lavatories. Beyond the
end of the platform was a ramp leading down to rail level, and as we
reached it, the engines deafened us with their whistles, and shot steam
into their cylinder cocks. The whole train rumbled past us. Then we left
the dry station for the open quay, with its luggage vans, its 0-6-0 'P'
class shunter and the French steamer *Invicta*, alongside. All the porters
dressed up like sailors so that it was hard to grasp who belonged
where, or even to realize the ship was French until you were aboard,
the stern flag hidden by that other Southern institution, the level luffing crane. And perhaps, most Southern of all, as the ship sailed we
saw the train, resplendant Pullmans and all, far out along the pier, as
if to show that, if it did not in fact run all the way to Calais, at least it
used those inconguous rails, set in the stone work half a mile out to sea!
Behind us, the cranes on their special tracks, straddling the quayside
railway line used by luggage vans, bent over the gangways, ready for
the next steamer. 'Stodhert & Pitt, Bath, England. Level Luffing
Crane', proclaimed cast iron notices on their jib counterweights, for us
to read from the ship, on either side of the cranedrivers corrugated iron
cabin, high above the rail track. So don't knock the Southern, the
cranes have long been swept away, with the rail track, to make a road,
and there is nothing like this today on the Admiralty Pier, since Dover
was electrified, and the Customs Hall has replaced the tracks. Today's
gangways are electrically operated and of course Dover has fallen over
itself to accommodate the all conquering juggernaut. Most sensible
people will have preferred the way we travelled all those years ago.

Chapter Six

Winchester 1930

The Southern Electric brought with it urban sprawl, and profits for Sir Herbert Walker's Board of Directors. 'Live in Surrey, Free from Worry; Live in Kent and be Content'. Maybe Network South East should reproduce the second of these posters, once their precious Networker trains have arrived!

Anybody could put up a house, there were no planning controls. Ribbon development proceeded apace but the non electrified Southern continued to run through the prettiest parts of England, where there were few factories, unlike today, with works polluting the area in many places, or looking hideous anyway. There are still large isolated patches of countryside left for the urban preservationists who know nothing of country ways, though their green wellies (they have to be green, ordinary folk wear black ones) are obvious enough. The gangers did not just keep the track weed-free, they cut the undergrowth, the alders, brambles, hazelbushes and sometimes gorse that are indigenous to Hampshire, Sussex and Kent, to minimise the risk of fire from locomotive sparks.

London's sprawl has been almost linked to the sprawl of the south coast's seaside towns by the rise of new towns in the middle, such as Basingstoke and Crawley. Now that the Basingstoke line has been electrified, the new towns have attracted many commuters, and also national institutions, like the Civil Service Commission.

In days gone by a trip to Bournemouth was a bit of an adventure, but since it was electrified over twenty years ago it is now just another commuter line. Somehow or other Southampton, unlike all the other important towns in what used to be the Southern Region, has kept a non-stop service which runs from Southampton Parkway, that station built to serve the airport originally, but which is near the M27. Fast trains from there to London are obviously intended to lure some motorists off the motorways. One has today to visit northern France to see what southern England used to look like, in spring for instance, bursting with banks of primroses, easily found cowslips to make cowslip wine, and of course woods awash with bluebells.

Life in the area consisted of farming, hunting, shooting, and fishing, and where it bordered on the commuterland, golfing. The towns were market towns, like Basingstoke and Alton, quite small, and of course Winchester itself, its huge diocese still stretching from the Berkshire border to Jersey, is steeped in history as William the Conqueror's capital and it possesses the longest Cathedral in Britain. Yet there was one other feature of life in the area about which not much was heard, preparatory schools.

Anyone who has not suffered, at the age of eight plus, these purgatorial institutions, cannot fully understand them. They have or anyhow had, something of the unfairness of treatment given to political prisoners. The only difference was that people paid to shut you up in the establishments, and that you were expected to like the ghastly atmosphere. The only blessing, was the escape, three times a year. I was incarcerated in Bereweeke Road, Winchester in 1930, a 'pre-preparatory school' available to eight to nine years olds.

'Pay attention to the game' is as vivid a memory of summer afternoons as the 'King Arthurs', passing in stately progress across the embankments of the Bournemouth main line, north of Winchester Station. Every other over was all right, but the best trains, perhaps even with a 'Lord Nelson' at their head, always seemed to go by when one's head was turned away from the line, in order to watch the confounded ball. Interminable cricket, wasting all those summer afternoons, was made tolerable by those Atlantic Liners, conveniently sailing from Southampton at about 4.30 pm, and so causing every possible path between the Bournemouth expresses, to be filled with boat trains.

The toiling procession of Drummond 4-4-0s, the 'K10s' with their tall chimneys, the 'L11s' with the boiler even higher, their appearance more gaunt and Scottish, and of course an enormous piece of running plate over the front of the bogie in front of the smokebox door, were the same mystery engines my father never explained on that Micheldever visit. Then those other Drummond 4-4-0s, with vast driving wheels nearly 7ft, the 'Greyhounds' of the system as the 'T9s' were called, sparks flying out of the chimney, though you could scarcely see them from the playing field, as they rushed up towards London and Micheldever Tunnel. Then there were the 'D15s', with tiny little chimneys and a decent forward window in the cab, rocking wildly as they ran downhill toward Winchester Station.

My ideas of engines were not 4-4-0s but 4-6-0s, and, sure enough, a thumping great 'T14' Paddlebox came flashing by, in a glorious kaleidoscope of gleaming green paint contrasting with that enormous black casting for outside cylinders and smokebox – green paint on engines and carriages alike, remote, mysterious, unfriendly, gaunt and hustling, full of sad army officers returning overseas for a two year duty, and tearful spouses about to bid goodbye. Except that some did not flash by at all, they fairly crawled, as an 'L11' struggled manfully in front of them with those luggage vans that distinguished SR van trains from all other railways. There were goods trains, too. Coal for various destinations, including, no doubt the Liners' bunkers. Many of the trains of covered vans, bringing imports and exports to and from Southampton Docks were hauled by 'N' class 2-6-0s, respectable looking 'Moguls' designed by Maunsell, and built largely at Woolwich Arsenal. The square Belpaire firebox and the slightly tapered boiler of these engines were a well tried feature elsewhere. Mr Maunsell's team had largely learnt their profession there, English engines, Swindon-style.

All the same, there were plenty of tiny 0-6-0s on several of the goods trains that looked as though the loads were really too much for them, for they only had to go to, or from, Basingstoke where they handed over their trains to the GWR for the run north. By contrast the GWR never seemed to run any of their own engines through from Reading to Portsmouth whenever I was on that unmentionable cricket field, although one boy took me out for the afternoon with his family, and feeling miserable, we went to Winchester SR station where every single train seemed to have a GW 2-6-0 on it.

Unfortunately the miserable playing field was so far off you could not see if the 'King Arthurs' had nameplates, let alone what they were. So maybe they were not 'Arthurs', but Mr Urie's 'H15s' or Maunsell's 'S15' mixed traffic engines which came in so handy for peak period boat trains. The crack train in early summer 1931 was the non Pullman 'Bournemouth Limited' of 1929. The name was revived for the first steam train from Waterloo to Bournemouth since 1967, on 11th September 1992. There were no Pullmans except boat trains and specials before July 1931. Maybe my memories are wrong, because I could have sworn the Up 'Bournemouth Belle' was the highlight of the day, especially as stumps were usually, belatedly, drawn soon after its passage. But I do not recall if it was wicked or not to play cricket on Sundays, after 5th July, 1931 when the famous 'Belle', then new, started. It did not run daily in 1931, only in 1936. The down train had gone before we emerged from the school buildings. The 'Bournemouth Belle' did not have new cars, but it broke new ground running on the Western Section, no doubt because Pullman had, the previous year, brought Pullmans to Torquay, and the rivals and rival resort, had to be challenged.

I personally believe Sir Herbert Walker thought Pullmans were rather a brash elegance, but much more likely the contract with Spiers and Pond for running the Western Section diners precluded Pullmans from that Section until it ran out. Wrongly no doubt, I imagined that the very wealthy Bournemouth residents, who managed even to get compartments in the first class part of the Wessex electrics in the 1980s when BR detested compartments, were too superior for the Pullmans of the Brighton line or the flamboyant Eastern Section to the Continent, where people went for a weekend flutter at Le Touquet, or longer indulgence at Monte Carlo, casinos being banned in Britain.

1930 when the slump began to hit, found the railways in an optimistic state though many of those trains hauled by *Sir Meliagrance, Sir Guy, Excalibur* and the rest, were probably half empty on their runs to Bournemouth. The 'S15s' were built by Maunsell to a modified 'Arthur' design. Saturday trains were better than ever, with disastrous results for the game, beloved by cricket masters, taking up our precious free time in the late afternoon.

Somehow the SR was firmly associated with unpleasantness. But I should not have knocked the Southern main line with its Drummond 4-4-0s, and its occasional GW train from the north to Portsmouth via Basingstoke, had I known what was in store in 1931. Instead of a mere twenty miles of the A34 road, up which we sometimes walked on the nice footpath set back from the highway, in the direction of Harestock. I was removed a further thirteen miles across the downs to the remotest, most beautiful and also the stuffiest part of Hampshire, where I usually felt ill. It was seven miles from the Portsmouth main line at Petersfield, not yet electrified of course, but that line did not make a junction with the line we could see from the school windows, any nearer than Woking.

If Mr Drummond's engines were gaunt, these were positively ghoulish, with square spectacle cab windows instead of round ones, and smokeboxes that sloped outwards towards the bottom. The wheel arrangement was not even 4-4-0, but 0-4-2, and as they were built by Mr Adams in 1887, of course they were called 'Jubilees' to celebrate Queen Victoria's fifty year reign. With the speed of a funeral train, they crept across the lofty viaduct over the river that gave the railway its name, a particular part of the Southern – the Meon Valley line.

Chapter Seven

Meon Valley Journey

Those ferocious porters who worked at West Meon station under a Stationmaster which gave it an importance it did not deserve, said that the line went Down to Fareham and Gosport. That you could change at Fareham for anywhere at all was never indicated, nor did Meon Valley railwaymen take any notice of anybody else. There was a bus to Southampton. Portsmouth could be reached by, bus from Fareham. Tales of woe were recited by those who had tried to change trains at Fareham. Indeed the late Charles Klapper, describing Sir Herbert Walker's marvellous ability to know vast numbers of his outside staff by sight as well as by name, chose Fareham as the scene where Sir Herbert appeared on the footbridge like a thundercloud, tall and furiosissimo behind those quivering pince-nez, commanding, 'Hold that train', to the Guard of the last Up Meon Valley train for Alton that was as usual about to start before the passengers from the Southampton train had time to board it. This was before my time, for by then there were no Sunday trains. The Guard was rightly summoned to appear before him at Waterloo on Monday morning when I think he was dismissed. This kind of discipline is what the proponents of railway privatisation would like to have restored in the 1990s. Discipline at preparatory schools was maintained with the cane, particularly if the headmaster was a sadistic pervert with a penchant for small boys, something my parents, anyway, never discovered. Luckily I was not well proportioned or good looking like his favourites, who suffered unmercifully at any transgression.

The blessed escape from this institution meant a journey over the Meon Valley line, the part that did not follow the *Meon*, so the very name was erroneous in my eyes. The station was nearly two miles away from the school and one and a quarter miles from the village. It was reached by passing under the great four arch steel viaduct that looked a hundred feet high but was only sixty-two, which dominated the valley. Hunt among the roadside nettles and you may still find the concrete base blocks. From West Meon village you climbed a lane which eventually crossed the line at the station on an overbridge which hid the water column from the imposing station house, which was at one time vandalised after abandonment. There was a lengthy passing loop, a small goods yard behind the house where local merchants received trucks of domestic coal and animal feed for farmers, but there any ressemblance to other, ordinary branches ended.

For the platforms were enormous, easily accommodating ten or twelve coach trains which never came – except on the very last day. The Railway Correspondence and Travel Society ran their special 'Hampshireman' Up the line from Fareham to Alton, stopping thirteen minutes for the two 'T9s' 30301 and 30732 on the front, to take water before the climb at one in one hundred through the waterless downs to Alton. The enthusiasts took pictures, and for me it was appropriate that the last train was an Up one, for I never went Down the line. I returned to the hated place by car, in sad isolation at the back. The railway had lasted a mere fifty-two years, when the last train ran on 6th February 1955.

Meon Valley trains were comprised of about three coaches, for the simple reason that any more would probably have defeated the 'Jubilees' utterly and completely. At one point the platforms sank to ground level to accommodate an occupation crossing and enable passengers to reach the Down platform, for the SR had removed the footbridge, possibly for use elsewhere on lines now fitted with the lethal third rail. The platforms had no view of the Up home signal, half hidden by another bend in the cutting to the south, and the Up starter was not lowered until the train arrived; in any case it was hidden by the overbridge leading to the station.

The cuttings deadened the sound of an approaching train, which crept up, shrouded in mystery, until suddenly there it was, wheezing and panting beside the great platform. The 0-4-2s often had 4-wheel tenders in those days, which I thought existed only on my Hornby clockwork layout, making the 'Jubilees' seem even more antediluvian than they really were, for they outlasted many other engines. Some were going strong well into BR days, though not on the Meon Valley after the line from London to Alton was electrified. At last we sallied forth from the station, round the bend and onto the famous viaduct, and if you think it has taken an eternity just to get out of West Meon, that is precisely how it seemed.

I believe Nos. 625 and 628 were the regular performers but would not swear to it. They were built by Neilson and Company for the LSWR in 1893 to Mr Adams' design. One would sedately trundle across the right hand side of the famous viaduct which had no track laid on the left, though everything was designed for double track throughout. In retrospect I feel it is possible that due to this lopsided arrangement for thirty years, by the time I travelled, there was some speed restriction which stopped the poor drivers getting a run at the hill.

To the right you had a pretty view of the *Meon*, a few feet wide, coming from East Meon, and its 17th century mansion standing in a capacious park, which looked a haven of tranquility. This was, in fact, my prison, and preparatory schools are best compared to foster homes run by councils or junior remand centres than anything else, in those days. Among other things, just to look out of the window at passing trains during classes was strictly forbidden, and the two relatively new Hants and Dorset bus routes, that passed the entrance down the road from East Meon and abstracted all the SR's local traffic, also had to be looked at in secret. One knew the bus times and when briefly to look up. Trains were more difficult.

One bus ran straight over the downs to Winchester, the county town, to which most people went on official business. This was far quicker than round by Alton, or Butts Junction where there was no station, so you had to retrace your steps there, to reach Winchester via Alresford, on the now preserved 'Watercress Line', shut west of Alresford and torn up.

The other route ran from West Meon through the valley villages of Warnford, Soberton and Meonstoke to Droxford, just like the railway, but the SR did not even bother to provide any of them with so much as a halt. The next station was 'Droxford, for Hambledon'. But Hambledon was several miles off to the east. There Southdown had a small garage in the village. Direct buses ran to Portsmouth and South-ampton, the latter omitting Fareham altogether. In those days of slump, the cheap Southampton shops were the goal of the poorly paid masters on their occasional half days off. No one in the school could afford a car, though the headmaster had two splendid Dennis motor mowers, one for the house and the other for the playing field across the road and up a lane, where you could hear, but not see trains. Just as well, in view of the dire penalties for not enjoying games.

Beyond the viaduct, our train would plunge into West Meon tunnel under this playing field ridge. The tunnel was 538 yards long with a curve to make it dark. Choking smoke would come thrusting through the window if we forgot to shut it, and the dim lights of the LSW thirds gave these tunnels an eerieness. But often there were no lights at all, and then the boys could enjoy themselves with some more of the bully-ing that they practiced in term time. No escape to the lavatory, as at school, the trains were non-corridor.

We emerged from the cutting where you could hear the trains from the playing field, onto an embankment sixty-four feet above the main A272 Winchester-Petersfield road whose underbridge was 167 ft long, more like a mini road tunnel! It was still standing in 1975, twenty years after closure of the line, but maybe its gone now as it was pretty narrow by modern road standards.

After this came Privett Tunnel, 1078 yards long, with an 'S' bend in it to make sure it was dark inside. To this day the cross roads where the A272 intersects the A32 from Fareham through West Meon to Alton, a mile north of the village, is called West Meon Hut. People thought this was because there was an AA box there, but it was named after the navvies' huts where they lived for six years, excavating these tunnels and building these huge viaducts, all by hand with picks and shovels, though later steam navvies were used on the cuttings.

After this, the train stopped at Privett station. This was also miles from anywhere, but not named after the bushes used for hedgemaking that grow wild in Hampshire, but after the 'nearby' village. Here the SR had reduced the place to the status of a halt. The large signal box was simply a ground frame after 1923, the only signals two fixed distants helping drivers after dark to realise they had to stop. The Up platform loop became a siding, like the rest of the goods yard.

Exactly why the LSWR decreed to build this line to double track on a ruling grade of only one in a hundred, has never been clear. It is true their main line to Portsmouth via Havant was only leased, and meant running over the LBSCR to Fratton using the lessor's running powers, which resulted in that famous battle of Havant with an LBSCR engine chained to the rails. The line was only seven miles away from the Portsmouth one at West Meon, but maybe seven miles was a long way in horse days. It was much shorter to Portsmouth than round by Basingstoke and Eastleigh to Fareham, but at least from Fareham, the rails into Portsmouth were their own to Cosham and jointly owned into the terminus at Portsmouth Harbour.

The line from Fareham to Gosport, opposite Portsmouth Harbour was older, and entirely LSWR. By far its most famous passenger was Her Majesty Queen Victoria who used it to reach the Royal Yacht *Alberta* for her journeys to and from Osborne House, on the Isle of Wight. Years went by before I discovered that the reason she spurned the station at Gosport, was that the station was inland, whereas the line went on to the quayside of the Royal Victualling Yard, an Admiralty establishment used for supplying food and other vital necessities to the Royal Navy's ships in the harbour.

Thus the spurious story grew up that the enormous unused platforms on the Meon Valley line were for Her Majesty's Ladies in Waiting to walk along the Royal Train, while the engine was watered, to reach Her Majesty who disapproved strongly of corridor coaches. Dire stories were told of how the ladies had to be pushed up into the train at Beattock on the 'Caledonian', during the Queen's long passages to Balmoral from Gosport, because the platforms were not long enough there, not quite nice in Victorian days of long skirts and petticoats. Maybe it was thought Her Majesty might go this shorter way to Windsor or even London, during one of her rare visits to Buckingham Palace, but she died before the line was completed in 1903.

Lurching off again from Privett, the 'Jubilees' eventually arrived at the end of the seven mile long section from West Meon, at Tisted (for Selborne). The SR did nothing to promote Jane Austen's long time abode at nearby Chawton as a tourist attraction or that of the great naturalist Gilbert White at Selborne. BR made up for this with their delightful 1957 film, *Journey into Spring*, made of course after Tisted was shut to passengers. At Tisted we met the Down pick-up goods, usually with an Adams '0395' class 0-6-0 which looked very similar to his 'Jubilees', one of which often substituted for the 0-6-0s on the goods. Occasionally a more modern Drummond '700' 0-6-0 whose boiler ressembled those on 'T9s', though it was not the same, would appear on the service. More potential traffic was abstracted here this time by Aldershot and District, who ran to Alton on certain days a week. On the way they served Faringdon village, which the SR had ignored until 1931 or so. The place had a small wooden ground frame serving sidings for local goods trucks. But in 1931 the SR decided to give it a halt. Passengers had to travel next to the engine, for this place could only accommodate a single coach. The platform had a single ramp at one end, and a step ladder at the other vertical end. The surface of the platform was mud. Farringdon was one of those places renamed by the railways. In 1934 the SR bestowed an extra 'r' on it, to distinguish it from Faringdon, Berkshire, now Oxon, which had a GWR branch, from Uffington.

About here the old 'Jubilees' speeded up a bit, as it was down hill, before climbing to join the 'Watercress' line at what was once a pair of double line junctions, the second lot leading to the Basingstoke and Alton Light Railway. The SR obliterated this, turning the two tracks to Alton into a double single, and removing the Basingstoke and Alton Light Railway which had already been removed once, in World War I. The film *Oh Mr Porter* was made on this line after closure but before the line was lifted. More poignant, the Meon Valley train staggered into Alton and reposed with the exhausted 'Jubilee' at its head, on one side of the island platform. The SR obligingly ran the London train onto the opposite face, instead of our having to climb the footbridge to the Up platform. All change.

The London train would have a *King Arthur* on it quite often. It had grand main line carriages with 'Waterloo, Southampton and Bournemouth' roof boards, and I could never understand why such a grand train was sent down the Winchester-Alton single line to collect us, indeed I never knew there was a Winchester-Alton railway until I first sampled the Meon Valley line. There was something incongrous about all those people from Bournemouth and Southampton having to wobble all round here to collect us. The Southern did not approve of this arrangement, all too like the 'Great Way Round', and got rid of it as fast as possible. Within two years of my last trip, they had electrified to Alton. At the end of summer term 1932, the 'Waterloo Express' arrived behind a 4-4-0 instead of a 4-6-0. How backward, I thought. The GWR had long ago stopped using such a wheel arrangement on important trains and scrapped its 'County' class 4-4-0s, except of course for those needed for the journeys between Bristol and Gloucester, where the line belonged to the LMS, who would not let the GWR use anything larger or heavier, claiming that the viaduct at Stonehouse would not stand it!

While I turned up my nose, it turned up even more at the excitement caused by the appearance of E910 *Merchant Taylors*; because it was brand new! Whether Eastleigh were running it in or checking it out prior to letting it loose on the Bournemouth main line was not determinable by a schoolboy. The angular cabs and large boilers two features that combined to operate on the Charing Cross-Hastings line with its narrow loading gauge, gave these engines a powerful appearance. The were of course every bit as good as an 'Arthur'. But 'Arthurs' were not Mr Maunsell's 4-6-0s, as most people know. He merely improved upon Urie's design whereas the 'Schools' and the 'Lord Nelson' 4-6-0s had this grand demeanour about them. After the pipes, and the ridiculously small cabs, and mysterious domes on top of the boilers of the great 'Pacifics' of the Nord of France, the 'Nelsons' appeared stately. And yet it was typically Southern, I thought, to name the 4-4-0s after famous public schools, since I detested all schools. The idea, was that of Sir John Elliot. Sir John had been to Marlborough, a place intended for sons of the clergy, but which produced rather famous eccentrics like Sir John Betjeman, and less famous ones too. (Readers of *Gone with Regret* and indeed this book can draw their own conclusions from this remark). Was it due to Elliot's education that the SR continued to run a through carriage at beginning of term, from Waterloo to Marlborough via Andover Junction, where the GWR took it over. Did the Southern have to threaten to use its running powers over the Midland & South Western Junction, to get it accepted? The horrors of public schools were what the terrors of preparatory schools were all about, preparing you for them, though of course getting pupils through the Common Entrance Examination was what they really meant. Most schools accepted this standard, why it was called Common was something never explained because Winchester College, which thought itself to be superior in every way, being the oldest in England, insisted on its own examination. Moreover it was the 'local' public school and our disgusting headmaster had been educated there. So the idea of reminding you of the beastly places when you were on holiday enjoying nice trips by train seemed to me, anyhow, typically Southern.

Compared to the Meon Valley train, which I believe went on as a slow to Guildford or Woking, the London train had fine carriages and a good turn of speed. But it stopped everywhere. It was not my idea of an express at all. First stop was Bentley, where people changed for Camp Bordon. Another piece of Southern mystique, why not call it Bordon Camp? And even more mysterious was the Longmoor Military Railway which started at Bordon Camp, though apparently military passengers had to go the other way (via the SR Portsmouth main line) to Liss, to which it was said to run through. Small groups and individuals were always conveyed to Liss by a Longmoor Military Railway railbus, but there was no physical connection with the Portsmouth line there, until the first week of World War II. SR trains worked regularly as required over the LMR for troop movements via Bordon. The route to South-ampton Docks for Movements Staff posted overseas was usually via Bordon, Bentley, Frimley Junction and Farnborough, starting from Longmoor Downs, the base depot.

'Camp Bordon' was an optical illusion, as close scrutiny of the official SR map will reveal that the word 'Camp' is slightly in italics, but appearing immediately above the word 'Bordon', also in capitals which creates the impression made. Nevertheless I am almost certain, that at Bentley, the porters used to shout 'Change here for Camp Bordon' (and there was never any mention of any Longmoor Downs extension, let alone a service of which there was none). The LMR line was a milit-ary secret and it was said that near Liss it was frequently not there, the track having been lifted and then relaid as a military exercise, for the Royal Engineers railway troops who trained there. Still secret at the time of my travelling, after World War II I did manage a visit to see *Gazelle* (part of the collection mentioned in Chapter Nine) on a plinth in the Officers Mess entrance. Now it has all disappeared and *Gazelle* is in the National Railway Museum at York.

Bentley remains, now famous as *The Village* in the BBC Radio series of that name. After Bentley the country changes to the sandy gorse and heather of Surrey. Our train stopped at Farnham, the first town after Alton and people would get in, so it was necessary to suck sweets and generally look as unattractive as schoolboys usually can, so as to repel boarders in our compartment. We were actively encouraged in this by the accompanying master who at any other time would have severely disapproved of our ungentlemanly behaviour.

After Farnham came Aldershot Town, so called because there is (I think still) Aldershot Government sidings, which was a military sta-tion. Then after that Ash Vale and its equally mysterious junction for Frimley and Ascot, used by trains from Aldershot.

Then the Pirbright Junction which is a flyover in a wood so you can hardly see it, and after emerging onto the four track main line from Basingstoke, the train stopped again at Brookwood, thereby relieving any main line trains from doing so I suppose. Brookwood was described as the station for Bisley, and great arguments ensued as to whether there really was a train to Bisley. All was explained about the shooting, and the national rifle competitions run for all and sundry; nothing was explained at all as to whether there was a military line to Bisley Camp, nor why was it called Bisley Camp instead of Camp Bisley, or whether it was an SR one. It appears to have been military line, but run by the SR for military freight traffic, and troop trains only.

If I remember rightly, the train then ran non stop to Waterloo. I sup-pose at Brookwood, the branch to the private station was still there, belonging to the London Necropolis Company Limited, who also had a private station at Waterloo and ran funeral trains from there to their vast Brookwood Cemetery. From the map, reversal at Brookwood was necessary, perhaps. There was no need to stop at Woking, as the place was served by the Portsmouth line trains. Guildford could be reached from Farnham, also Aldershot so nobody wanted to change.

After Woking the thrill of Brooklands racing track, then Weybridge, where London General buses thoughtfully put in an appearance. The single deck rear entrance 'T' type were rare birds, never seen in Central London. Near Tolworth, or rather near Surbiton station there were the London United's trolleybuses, known as 'Diddlers' to bus enthusiasts, but equally rare birds, also they were pretty new at the time. I made numerous trips before discovering where to look for several buses ending their long journeys across London at the *Junction Tavern*, beside Raynes Park Station.

The excitement of London had begun, and soon there was to be the intricacies of Clapham Junction to look forward to. The mysteries of the Southern Electric, trains dashing about everywhere, in more frequent numbers, it seems to me, than nowadays, paled into insignificance before the exciting prospect of escaping from the vigilant eye of the master in charge of the party. But of course the Southern was on his side, so naturally after Vauxhall we stopped: stuck outside the station, actually waiting for an electric train to cross all the main lines so as to be ready to return from the Down slow at Platforms 1 & 2. The master had time to give us a last minute harangue about good behaviour on the platform, wearing school caps and so forth. How was I to guess what they hoped for was that our superb deportment and our caps would advertise the school to prospective parents as well as to our own, who had come to meet us. How well I remember the first time our train sailed into Waterloo non stop, before the master had time to give his last minute lecture which so spoilt the pleasure of the vast numbers of trains on the outer edge of the great station, the 'Atlantic Coast Express' among them, ready to leave.

Now one could forget those dreadful bullying boys who knew all about how the Navvies, who built the Meon Valley line, chastised one of their number who had committed some social crime, by stripping him to the waist and beating him with stinging nettles. If you live in Hampshire, you will know that nettles there grow four feet high and have three inch stinging leaves, while the quarter inch stem can give you a nasty sting too. Luckily the opportunity to strip boys to the waist and beat them with nettles was never able to arise. The nettles were there all right and the stripping off for bathing in the filthy muddy *Meon*. The headmaster built a second pool as the first had somewhat silted up, being simply a widening of the river, dammed up. Here the boys could dive, but it was in full view of the road. This worried the headmaster not one whit. To see his boys stark naked in the pool was one of his delights and he took care not to miss it, consequently there

Petersfield, L.S.W.R., 1919

was no chance for boys to get nettles.

The return to the place, sad, lonely and by road, always included an SR 'M7' 0-4-4 tank, waiting at Winchester Cheesehill GW station for a train from Newbury – a reminder already that holidays and home were left behind, for the last glimpse of the GWR, only disclosed this trespassing SR tank.

But in 1934 I had an accident on Guy Fawkes night when we had to go into the park at night to watch the fireworks. The sparklers were particularly handy for the bullies. I slipped on the bank and fell against the flint wall supporting the edge of the lawn, giving the appearance of a continuous piece of green stretching far away into the park, as seen from the house, an arrangement called a Ha Ha. I damaged my nose permanently, and my lip required stitching. I was seriously hurt, or anyway my parents arranged my early escape or possibly the school did not want the trouble of me in the sick bay for many weeks. Anyhow I escaped, and my mother assured my headmaster I was quite capable of travelling alone. However she was not capable of realising that a train from Petersfield was a Portsmouth one, and was looking for trains from West Meon. Maybe the stupid authorities had not told her they put me on the Petersfield train, so as not to change at Alton, and anyway my parents not the school would have had to pay for the taxi.

So I found myself on Petersfield station, of which I have a nice drawing on a Christmas card by Hamilton Ellis with LSWR steam, such was his great love, close to the level crossing which was also the boundary between the Hants & Dorset and the Southdown. The train of non corridor carriages and an antideluvian Drummond 4-4-0 with Urie stovepipe chimney to make it more sinister and antiquated, came trundling in. How was I to know the line would soon be electrified? There were no Pullmans on LSWR trains, nor diners either. Later, on steam-hauled main lines there would be Mr Bulleid's frightful Tavern Cars, out of which you could not see, in the hope that this would encourage you not to linger, and either drink up and have another, or make space for others. A Pullman habitué like me never set foot in a Tavern Car. I believe that they were craftily introduced by Oliver Bulleid, the SR's poetic and inventive Chief Mechanical Engineer, who succeeded Maunsell, while Sir John Elliot was on secondment in Australia. E. C. Cox, the SR's Traffic Manager from 1923, previously with SE&CR, who was violently opposed to alchohol, refused to allow any buffet cars in the new 1937 Alton and Portsmouth electric trains. The eleven year old boy looked astounded at the 4-4-0 was it a 'K10'? 'Is this the London train' he haughtily asked the porter. Remember in 1934 there were Hall 4-6-0s on the GWR as well as 'Saints'; with 'Castles' and 'Kings' for the long distance trains. 'Course it is. What D'yer think it was?' 'Where I come from, with an engine like that on it, I thought it was for the Midhurst Branch'. Furious, the porter bundled me into a compartment. Midhurst branch trains were anyway consigned to a bay on the wrong side of the level crossing, I seem to recall. This was minus any amenities, the passengers having a long wet walk. As Southdown occasionally ran their 59 bus, which was a Tilling-Stevens single decker such as we encounter elsewhere in these pages, it was not so surprising that the Midhurst branch train seldom ran and did not pay, while the bus met its costs by running through to Bognor. Southdown's double deck Leylands to Portsmouth were far more frequent, and only electrification won back some of the traffic.

The 4-4-0 inched its way up to Haslemere, passing Liss where the Longmoor Military Railway ran through regularly during World War II. The train also passed Liphook, where the Military Railway serving the Ordnance Depot was a bit more conspicuous. But memories of this journey are blurred by the non-presence of my mother at hateful Waterloo, and I could not understand what had become of her. I was silly enough not to realise that she could not distinguish the total difference between a train arriving from Portsmouth, and one arriving from Bournemouth and Southampton via Alton, and thought she had been killed. No such odious thoughts were ever encountered at Paddington as eventually, she turned up at the Train Arrivals Indicator.

No mention of Portsmouth would be complete without remarking on the Dockyard or the Isle of Wight, for which latter purpose, Portsmouth Harbour was built, extending the railway at a different level to the terminal platforms of Portsmouth & Southsea which you do not suppose is actually in Southsea, but in central Portsmouth.

Portsmouth, Devonport and Chatham Royal Naval Dockyards all had their own fascinating but strictly secret internal railway systems, all connected to the Southern. But Royalty leaving for the Empire in one of His Majesty's ships, usually embarked in Portsmouth where there was another mystery place called South Jetty. Linked to this was a floating landing stage, whose holystoned oak decking shone as well as any battleship's wooden decking. In it was a line of rails reached by a bridge connection with a weight limit on it. So the pictures of the 'Royal Train', usually formed of Pullman Cars on the Southern, rushing down to Portsmouth are steam hauled, often by a 'T9' Drummond 4-4-0, as nothing heavier could use the Dockyard line. There are pictures of Kings and Queens reviewing Naval Ratings with both a ship and a train in the background but photographs of its coming or going are rare.

HMS *Victory*, Lord Nelson's 1805 Flagship is preserved in the dockyard, the Naval Base is also called HMS *Victory*, and the public have always been graciously allowed to enter the private world of the Royal Navy, to view it. It is of course a right and proper place to take young boys, and one fine day we were carted off by motor car to see it. The great ship and its rigging were shown off to us, while the Authorities pretended that the Dockyard and its Railway were not really there. However the first crane engines I ever saw appeared there as did half a dozen or so little Admiralty 0-4-0Ts. The Dockyard lines had fantastic curves, the tracks all laid in the roadways. Mostly they only took one wagon, or sometimes even a piece of ship's fitments would come by, dangling on the end of the engine's crane. It was fascinating to watch, and the Admiral's quarter deck gave a superb view. The authorities however considered this interest in secret railways and little engines rather than ship's rigging, to be quite diabolical. Healthy boys liked rugger, not miserable steam engines. so we were grabbed and dragged below to see the great Admiral's cabin, where he died; which of course was totally without interest, to the chagrin of those in charge. Possibly nowadays the existence of the Dockyard lines, some traces of which can still be found, is no longer a secret, now crane engines can no longer come round blind corners with piercing shrieks on their steam whistles.

The Southern is permanently associated with mystery lines into equally mysterious stations belonging to the Government, built ever so long before the SR was nationalised. One adjoined the Royal Naval Barracks at Portsmouth into which recruits could be sent by ordinary SR trains, specially chartered, without fear of desertion or 'jumping ship' I suppose it would be called, even though the 'ship' was just SR thirds. Sometime back the existence of the now defunct Devonport Dockyard railway was disclosed, so long it even ran workmen's passenger trains.

Secret trains on secret railways are the heart of the SR mystique. And even if Queen Victoria never lived to travel on the Meon Valley line, it had its moment of glory in 1944. General Eisenhower's headquarters before D-Day were at Southwick House, in Southwick Village near Fareham, a village whose pub was one of the last to brew its own beer. There was, you will recall, a great but secret row among the top people of Britain because His Majesty King George VI announced his intention of leading his ships into action on this momentous invasion occasion. He had, of course served in action as a Midshipman at the Battle of Jutland. Winston Churchill refused to let him do so, but had every intention of accompanying Montgomery in his headquarters ship, something which Montgomery said was not feasible. Churchill took no notice and even less notice of Eisenhower's remarks about protection and responsibility for his safety being too much of a burden for Generals with the invasion on their hands. Eventually Churchill was dissuaded by Royal Command, but he was given the use of the 'Royal Train' as there was no room at Southwick for Churchill and his staff. So the 'Royal Train', with Churchill and several Cabinet Members aboard, proceeded stealthily down the Meon Valley line to Droxford, where it stabled in the goodsyard. Churchill and his entourage spent several nights in it there, linked by telephones to London. During the day he motored over to Eisenhower at nearby Southwick, and nobody could tell that this remote place with few facilities, was harbouring such VIPs.

In just over a decade later, the line shut to passengers. The viaduct yielded 700 tons of scrap, though goods trains continued until 1968 between Alton and Farringdon. The line was also open for goods from Knowle, where it met the Eastleigh-Fareham line, up to Droxford. The goods trains used Maunsell Moguls at both ends. Traffic to Droxford ceased in 1962 when the line was leased to a Mr Charles Ashby who had a railbus called a Sadler Pacerail. He hoped to introduce these on local lines, especially the Isle of Wight.

But Mr Ashby presumably did not realise that the *Meon* valley is full of rough rural people, and Hampshire was as harsh as it always was. Though Privett station is now a desirable residence in the stockbroker belt, worth many thousands, West Meon and Droxford stations were ruined by vandals, as was the diesel railbus. For a time 'A1X' SR 'Terrier' built by Stroudley for the LBSCR, No. 32646 and a US Army 0-6-0 Dock tank from Southampton Docks No. 30064 were stored at Droxford. The 'Terrier' is now on the Isle of Wight, after a long stay at Havant on a plinth, as a memorial to the *Hayling Billy*, the Hayling Island branch train. The wooden bridge leading onto the Island could take nothing heavier than a Stroudley 'Terrier'. The USA tank is now on the 'Bluebell Railway'. The track to Droxford lasted to 1969.

One night around midnight I was driving back from Glyndebourne in 1947 (Chapter Eleven) to my parents home at Newbury en route to a Cheltenham concert next day, when I was stopped at Fareham station level crossing. There was a long pause, and then a two-coach train came rushing past without lights. The coaches seemed older and with flatter roofs than the electric '2-BILS' I was used to seeing in Sussex at the time, and on the rear, as it sailed by, was an 'M7' 0-4-4 tank, its fireman shovelling lustily, outlined in the light of the firebox, running flat out around fifty miles an hour, making for its home shed at Guildford. All kinds of sinister ghostly memories swelled up as I waited for the signalman to open the gates; my passenger, tired from conducting the Opera, was asleep in the back. Starting the engine brought me back to reality, for I knew exactly what that ghost train was, the last Meon Valley train I ever saw.

Chapter Eight

The Asterisk in Bradshaw

A school friend was responsible for persuading me to go with him to the Hundred of Hoo, which sounded spooky and mysterious. Today its old Norman name is half forgotten, and it is called the Isle of Grain. Hundreds have pretty well died out, though when a Member of Parliament wishes to resign, he applies for the Chiltern Hundreds, which are supposedly somewhere in the Chilterns, like the Prime Minister's official country seat, Chequers. But there is surely no connection. The Hundred of Manhood is another which you will find in these pages, whilst if you visit the Island of Jersey you will find twelve Honorary Police Forces, one for each parish, and the Policemen are known as Centeniers, one for each Centaine (Norman French for Hundred) in each parish.

My friend was fascinated by the name, and by the 'asterisk' in Bradshaw. Much later the Isle of Grain was smothered in oil refining equipment and machinery and materials. It has also had brief fame as the place where all the concrete segments for lining the English portion at the Channel Tunnel were made. They were of course transported by Class '33' diesels to the site of the Tunnel at Shakespeare Cliff, and now the Tunnel is completed, the Isle has sunk back into its usual obscurity. But probably the new high speed line that the British Government has insisted shall go miles round by Rainham marshes instead of straight up to London from the Tunnel mouth, as any other country would have done, and got the line constructed in time for the Tunnel opening too, means that visitors to Britain will eventually get a brief glimpse of the Hundred of Hoo, as they whizz by at 300 kilometres an hour. I am now wondering if I shall live long enough to go on it!

In the 1930s, the Hundred of Hoo had atmosphere. Vying with Sheppey, cut off by *Thames* one way and *Medway* the other, the island projects into the *Thames Estuary*, a chunk of England overlooked somehow though you can see it quite well on clear days from the air if your aircraft is following the north or Essex Bank of the *Thames*. The *River Thames*, tidal all the way to London, thirty-eight miles off, is quite wide and salty in these parts. How was it Southend, with its pier sticking out a mile or more into the river, or Sheerness on the neighbouring Isle of

'The gateway to the continent, and all those buses as well!' The forecourt of Victoria Station about 1937. The 76A on the left was for Ponders End, the 16 on the right went to Cricklewood. *George Behrend Collection*

This is how the SR dealt with, 'the wrong sort of snow', a Stirling 'F' class 4-4-0 hauling an electric unit. *J. H. Price*

Going to the races, fifty years apart.

Above, S&ECR 'F' class 4-4-0 No. 183, built in 1892, heads a Folkestone Races special at East Croydon. *E. T. Vyse*

Below: **In the early 1950s a Charing Cross-Tattenham Corner Pullman Race Special is seen climbing Forest Hill bank, headed by 'N' class Mogul No. 31827.** *A. M. S. Russell*

Brighton engines at Brighton in the early BR period.

Above: **'K' class Mogul No. 32343.** *W. H. Butler Collection*

Below: **'An arrow pointing, with "Brighton" above, on a huge green board',** with **'C' class 0-6-0 No. 31227 in attendance.** *W. H. Butler Collection*

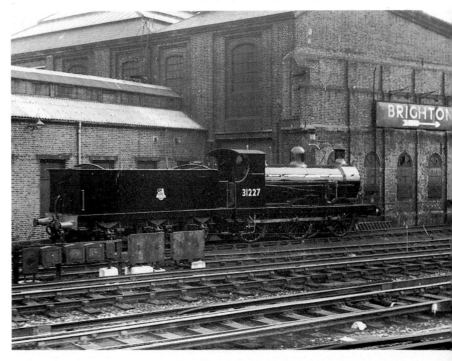

Cleaners are making a good job of 4-4-2T 32091, an '13' class engine built in 1913 and withdrawn in 1952. *W. H. Butler Collection*

Probably the most famous train on the Southern, 'The Golden Arrow', passing Bromley South in July 1929 headed by 'Lord Nelson' class 4-6-0 E864 *Howard of Effingham*.
A. M. S. Russell

The last steam hauled 'Golden Arrow' entering Platform 8 at Victoria on 11th June 1961 hauled by 'West Country' Pacific No. 34100 *Appledore*. *A. M. S. Russell*

Down 'Golden Arrow' at the remodelled Orpington Junction in 1959. The old alignment can be seen on the right. *A. M. S. Russell*

Riddles BR '7P Britannia' Pacific, No. 70004 *William Shakespeare* on the Down 'Golden Arrow' at Folkestone Warren in July 1952   *I Hanson*

The 'Southern Belle'.

Above: **In LB&SCR days headed by 'I3' class 4-4-2T No. 23.** *J. H. Price Collection*

Below: **Post grouping, the train is at Merstham hauled by ex LBSCR 'J' class 4-6-2T B325.**
W. H. Butler Collection

A well creased picture of West Meon viaduct looking towards West Meon village. The station was to the left, the tunnel to the right. *J. H. Price Collection*

An Edwardian view of Fareham station showing the footbridge from which Sir Herbert Walker stopped the departing Meon Valley train. *J. H. Price Collection*

An Adams 'Jubilee' No. 550 at Clapham Junction in LSWR days. This was the class that dominated services on the Meon Valley line during my period of incarceration in the vicinity. This one had round cab windows. *E. T. Vyse*

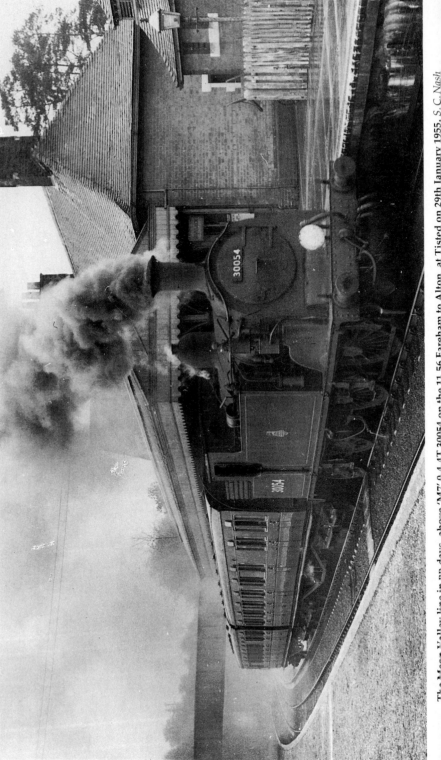

The Meon Valley line in its days above 'M7' 0-4-4T 30054 on the 11.56 Fareham to Alton, at Tisted on 29th January 1955. S. C. Nash

'T9' 4-4-0 No. 30730 pauses to shunt the 10.20 am Alton to Fareham freight, at West Meon on 19th November 1954. The lengthy platforms are clearly shown in this view. *S. C. Nash*

Drummond '700' class 0-6-0 No. 30325 heads the local goods out of Privett on 18th December 1954. *S. C. Nash*

Alton on 20th January 1973, with '4-VEP' Unit No. 7814 on a train to Waterloo and a Hampshire diesel electric unit, on the soon to be closed service to Winchester. Part of this line, as far as Arlesford, has been preserved to form the Mid Hants Railway. *J. H. Price.*

Sheppey, across the *River Medway*, could be happy holiday resorts for Londoners seeking a day by the sea, when Allhallows could not? A development was needed at Allhallows and, oh joy! no planning permission was needed to start it.

So the Southern were persuaded to build a new line from Stoke Junction to Allhallows-on-Sea, with a brand new terminal station boasting a long island platform, which opened on 16th May 1932. Stoke Junction was provided with a Halt on 17th July, presumably because most trains now went to Allhallows. Roger Kidner has written that the Southern ran through coaches from Cannon Street to Allhallows for a short time and that 6,500 passengers went to Allhallows on the August Bank Holiday of 1932. But developments suffer in times of slump, though trippers were enticed to enjoy Kentish estuarial mud as much as the Essex mud. Kidner says that tripper traffic grew enough for the line to be doubled from Stoke Junction, but with hindsight I suspect this was really to make it look attractive to commuters, who despite being urged to 'Live in Kent and be Content', did not materialise in large numbers. No one had ever heard of Allhallows-on-Sea, or anyhow, my friend and I had not. 'Let us go to this mysterious Port, named after Queen Victoria: the only trouble is,' he said, 'that there are only two trains a day, and the first one so early in the morning, we will never make it'.

The roads for Allhallows were laid out by the developers and Maidstone and District Motor Services were paid to run double deckers to Allhallows, to give it status. So we set off for Rochester. The famous Southern Electric, was not, until 1939 extended to Chatham and Gillingham from Bickley Junction, or from Gravesend. On arrival we ignored the hoards of buff coloured Chatham & District Traction double deckers, a subsidiary of the Maidstone Company, whose green buses all started from Gillingham with the exception of ours. The oil workers were conveyed from Gravesend by M&D's 17 service justifying double deckers, but Allhallows in the wet spring was a different story. Our bus was service 65 and when it came, to our astonishment it had a Leyland petrol engine and an open top!

We scrambled upstairs, covering our knees with the tarpaulin so thoughtfully provided in those far off, civilised days, and travelled in the misty rain over the bridge, past the Chattenden and Upnor Tramway (Deceased: Admiralty Property, No Admittance). So, on into Hoo's mysterious Hundred, while the conductor, sheltering inside the lower deck instead of underneath the stairs, thought we had eloped from either Hellingly or Park Prewett. Both these asylums, as the SR expert passengers will already know, had special branch lines. The Hellingly one worked by the establishment itself with its own petrol loco, the Park Prewett line was rarely used, except by the occasional antediluvian engine which crept up with a few truckloads of coal. Until its demise, the Basingstoke & Alton Light Railway's allotted locomotive usually performed this duty.

To return to our present adventure, we were of course the only passengers on the bus. Presently we gazed down on Allhallows magnificent station, on a few shacks and bungalows; on fields of couch grass run to seed too damp for sheep, too salty for cattle, but covered with a concrete road system. At one of the road junctions, our bus suddenly swung to the right, and plunged downwards. At a crazy angle, its front deep in the marsh, its rear still on hard concrete, we paused, awaiting what might happen next. The conductor politely told us that we must get off.

But, we protested, we were going on to Stoke. In that distinctive nasal tone that distinguished Kentish men (or is that Men of Kent?) from cockneys, it was courteously explained that of course we were, but that no one would go anywhere if the bus got stuck! The driver roared the engine of his Leyland Titan (TD1), while the conductor pranced like the Kentish heraldic white horse on the rear platform, and after some wheelspin, the front end lifted.

We pulled up in the road, facing the direction by which we had come upon this extraordinary brand new station with no visible trains. We knew it was called Allhallows only because of one of those round yellow AA signs, long disappeared, and the UDC notices that said so. Nobody got on; and we were the only ones around to get off. So we waited patiently on the rear transverse seats with the driver and conductor; while the engine roared, wasting petrol, vital that it should not stall, especially when the front end was in the mud, because there was no self-starter, and it must be swung by hand. (For those interested in buses, it was virtually identical to the preserved Southdown open top Leyland TD1 in Amberley Chalk Pits Museum garage, at times when Southdown are not using it themselves).

The driver kindly explained matters. Because the M&D had a contractual obligation to run double deckers, in winter they ran the open topped buses that in summer graced Hastings' Sea Front. The council and the developers were furious but impotent. It never dawned on the good people of Allhallows that M&D had such buses, tucked away in far off Sussex! Instead of ultra modern vehicles, they had a bus just as old-fashioned as the most decrepit single decker – and open top, too! The M&D were quite happy to provide these old things which would otherwise have been idle, and in store. In addition this saved wear and tear on their nice new diesel double deckers, and enabled one or two extra to go for overhaul, instead of running empty to Stoke. The driver looked at his watch, and got out; we dashed back upstairs again.

But this time our journey was quite short. We were deposited beside a level crossing, where there was a ground frame and a tin shelter. We enjoyed this comfort while our bus, long since, had returned to the relative bustle of Chatham. But this was not as other halts, though Southern corrugated iron seemed remarkably the same where ever it was to be found, this looked as though it had been around for years, instead of being barely five years old. For this was Stoke Junction Halt where trains normally ran on to the grand station at Allhallows, though sometimes they disappeared out of the timetable altogether, like the one we patiently awaited, which presently arrived. We did not buy a ticket, because no tickets were issued here.

The train, a two-coach push and pull, stopped, for the guard to unlock the ground frame. The driver was quite startled to see us climb aboard. The planks were slippery, the green, non-corridor coach's step quite high above it. The 'H' class 0-4-4 Tank engine whistled for our benefit. We trundled across the flat marshes over track ballasted with cinders. A quiet sigh came from the engine which was fitted with a Westinghouse air brake pump, as well as vacuum brakes and soon it stopped at the open platform – shown only as an 'asterisk' in the timetable. The other passenger in the train got out.

Port Victoria was a single platform halt. It had a nameboard. There was a single house and a coastguard cottage, to whom the train must have been a lifeline. (What has happened to it now?). Beyond the train lay mist, and also more lines which just here were double track, and a crossover, hand-operated as a run round loop, not needed by the autotrain.

We walked towards the wooden platforms beside these rails, and realised suddenly that all were on a wooden pier. The Guard delivered a parcel, bread, I presume to the SR's *Port Victoria Hotel*. This was an all wooden building, like the platform, and opened with the railway in 1882. Lit by oil lamps, there was no electricity at Port Victoria, it was really a refreshment room with bedrooms. Originally it was leased to H&G Simmonds, the Reading brewers (taken over eventually by Courage) and it lasted until 1952. 'Passengers must not pass this point' said a standard SR notice, one of the metal sort with raised letters. Underneath a hand painted notice in the same style but on a wooden board, read: 'You do so at your peril'. The Guard shouted at us to keep away from the Pier. It seemed extraordinary that this desolate place once had a boat train with a Pullman car, also hauled by a 0-4-4 tank, 'H' class or maybe 'R' class, connecting somehow with a ship to Holland, all started because the Queenborough Pier on Sheppey, had caught fire and was out of use. Port Victoria was the SER's answer to LCDR's Queenborough.

We returned to the train, but instead of a friendly chat, we were harangued by the driver, who was an ardent communist. It was a dour experience, and new; as dour as the pier was dank. Full of invective about wealthy young gentlemen in lovely public schools, the driver swept on. In vain we told him of the iniquities of such places and how we hated it, particularly the compulsory military parades, and the conscientious objection inquisition if you dared not to 'volunteer'. He would have none of it. How wicked was the inequality of education; how wicked was the unemployment; how wicked the waste of time, running to ludicrous dumps like Port Victoria, where no one, except rich young gents like us, who could afford to, would dream of going.

We pointed out that we had travelled free from Stoke, and added 'Single to Charing Cross please, twice.' 'You must be joking' said the Guard. Humbly, we said we had money, (how the driver sneered) and were quite willing to pay. 'Get your tickets at Beluncle' snapped the Guard. 'Can't you see this desolate platform has no booking office?'

The rain had stopped. We would have liked a photograph. The driver, offended deeply by two toffee-nosed capitalist schoolboys, would have none of it. He jumped into the end compartment of the carriage, and blasted on the whistle cord. At what was now the back of the train, nearest the Pier, the fireman stuck his head out of the cab, then whistled again, and clanked his shovel. With a lurch we started, rapidly and unemotionally across the desolate marsh, which I believe is now all part of the BP refinery. A new station for the workers was built, called Grain. The driver's lecture had upset us, for communism, like visiting Port Victoria, was not part of the Marlborough College syllabus.

We had never met a communist before. The driver tore along non-stop past Grain Crossing Halt and Middle Stoke Halt. Actually he was making up time to allow for us to buy our tickets at Beluncle, one of the intermediate stations between Stoke Junction Halt and the main line at Gravesend. But we were convinced that he would leave Beluncle early too, and as we were the last train, and the last bus had already gone, Hoo's ghostly marshy plain seemed even more menacing and eerie. Were there inns in such oddly named places as Wainscott and Beluncle? I imagined a night on a wooden bench in a pub, with sawdust on the floor. But luckily the porter in charge at Beluncle Halt seemed unperturbed by passengers dashing into his booking office to buy tickets, making sure that we were not left behind. We stopped briefly at Sharnal Street, with Admiralty exchange sidings for their Chattenden Tramway, and at Cliffe, a real station, missing out High Halstow and Uralite Halts, the latter named after some mineral. Presently the train seemed almost to lose its eerie character, rattling over Hoo Junction, and non-stop past Milton Range and Denton Halts to Gravesend, simply another SR suburban place, among familiar Southern Electric sets. We scuttled back to London and our comfortable homes, wondering what sort of back-to-back with one tap down the yard, our erstwhile driver lived in, at Chatham or wherever.

'The asterisk in Bradshaw'! The very name 'Bradshaw' is half forgotten now, as is the curious way that all the railway companies' public timetables were simply reprints from it, except of course the GWR who printed their own peculiar Timebook. These were quite different to those set out in Bradshaw. But Bradshaw too, had its own way of doing things. On the Southern there was a Table called 'The South Coast and London' although Southern south coast resorts like Folkestone or

Bournemouth could never be found in it. Why? Because it meant the London-Brighton and South Coast line. Another Table was grandly headed 'Waterloo and the West of England' assuming that you knew where Waterloo was and as though the Southern ran everywhere in the west. If you were not enticed into the wrong train by such misleading blandishments, then what about this extraordinary place not even worthy of a mention in the Allhallows-on-Sea branch Table, but marked merely as an 'asterisk', and a footnote explaining that the train concerned arrived or departed from Port Victoria four minutes later/ earlier or whatever it was. The journey retained an eerie portent of things to come. If I had known my history, I could have told the driver his big boss had run the railways in World War I, and thus Sir Herbert Walker had kept Port Victoria in case it was needed for emergencies. Though soon afterwards it was abandoned.

I was reminded of this journey when I went to the Farjeon Revue, called *Tuppence Coloured*. Revues have finished now, you never got the best of them unless you sat near the front, where you could hear the words. This was 1948, when Roland Emett's cartoons of grotesque steam engines were a national success. Max Adrian was a pillar of these Herbert Farjeon productions. Farjeon wrote most of it himself as well as producing the show. The last lines were pronounced in dirge-like manner. Sadly I have long forgotten all the verses except this one;

> 'Now all the Puffers
> Are run by old buffers
> In Whitehall, some people condemn it.
> But the're things you don't know
> On the Saturday Slow,
> Since they've nationalized Mr Emett's
> Which stops –
> If the 'asterisk' in Bradshaw is not at fault
> At Wysteria Halt'.

So don't knock the Southern, for BR cannot take you to Port Victoria today . . .

But history repeats itself. BP closed its huge Refinery in the 1980s. In the same decade roadstone began to be imported by sea to Grain from Scotland and was sent by rail to various sites. Trans Manche Link, builders of the Channel Tunnel have in 1992 abandoned the plant where they made all the segments that lined the tunnel in concrete.

So now there is a new commercial jetty or rather quay, 550 metres long that takes ocean going container ships rather than cross channel vessels. In 1992 a new container terminal has been started at right angles to the new quay, replacing a temporary one among the BP transfer sidings. The line from Hoo Junction is to have four freight trains a day, as well as those for the roadstone, and some residual BP traffic.

The place has the prosaic name of Thamesport – fifty years after Port Victoria was visited in its state of collapse. Now socialists and communists are on the wane in many parts of the world, it's simple to see that actually, the 'asterisk' in Bradshaw was really a symbol for being in advance of its time.

Chapter Nine

A Night in the Lord Warden

My father gave up his London *pied à terre* when the lease ran out. He did not like London so much as the country, whereas my mother was always a city person, never happier than when following the latest trends in art or music. The death of my grandmother, who domineered her son, gave the opportunity to abandon London for good, but never was the place missed by the family more, than when going abroad.

As no decent trains to Newbury from Paddington ran late enough to connect with our arrival on the boat train at Victoria, we were faced with the choice of an expensive hotel night in London on top of the holiday, or going home by car. Motoring was fine, but there was always the possibility of having a breakdown. My parents were so totally unversed in reliable 1930s motorcars that they expected break-downs. More to the point, the chauffeur from the country would have to find his way into Victoria's entrance alone, battle his way in, and meet the train correctly. And if it were late, or if for some reason we should not be on it, there was no means of communicating.

It often happened that people failed to turn up. Through trains from Austria and Switzerland which bore carriages on two or three days trips from Romania and Greece, or Turkey, often did not connect with the boat at Calais, which did not keep the Paris-London passengers waiting long. Instead through train passengers caught the next service.

I suppose my father learnt about the Birkenhead-Dover through train from me. He often used to take us for a picnic on the *Thames* at Pangbourne or near Goring and Streatley station, both locations offering nice views of the GWR main line to Bristol. The appearance of it, with its Maunsell Mogul trespassing onto the GWR as far as Oxford, did not go unremarked. So he had decided to try it. Four nights in Wagons-Lits were considered too much of a good thing, and anyway he did not wish to change trains in Paris, coming back from Switzerland. A night in Dover was much cheaper than London, and the attractive *Lord Warden Hotel* with its early Victorian architecture, followed by Dover's only train that did not go to London, was decided upon. He and my mother hated cross-channel steamers. In the summer of 1937 we made the out-ward journey on the 'Night Ferry' which meant that we could forget about the Channel altogether. But coming back was a different matter. A trip of fourteen hours in the train on the Continent was followed by the passage across the Channel. Add to this the boat train to London followed by the long journey home from there and it is easy to see why the return journey was much more fraught than the civilised convenience of the outward leg.

The *Lord Warden Hotel* was built by the LC&DR at the same time as the Admiralty Pier. It could have been designed for railway enthusiasts, as it had lines all round it! My father was not unduly worried by the noise. The tracks passed some distance from what is now 'Southern House'. The bridge and its approach embankment deadened the noise, and anyway my father liked the idea that the sea was outside the windows, close by. That the main line from Dover Marine, as 'Western Docks' was always called until the 1970s, to Folkestone and London was even closer, did not concern him, knowing it would please me, and that there was only one more boat train, that catering for passengers on the Ostend-London service, to pass after our own arrival, until the 'Night Ferry' came at midnight.

What he had not bargained for was the way the Southern worked Dover. First of all, alongside the Dover Marine main line and even nearer the sea, were sidings leading to Dover shed. The shed was just out of vision of the lounge windows, but there seems to have been no turntable, owing to the narrowness of the site and proximity to the sea.

Instead, the turntable was outside the smoking room and dining room windows, as were a number of sidings adjoining the double track main line from Dover Marine to Priory, Chatham and London, from which the line to Deal branched off at Buckland Junction north of Priory station. This area is now roadway and a lorry park. Its size can be seen by the presence of Dover Marine Signal Box, now well back from the single track which is all that remains. In the thirties, the Calais boat trains were seldom routed this way. My parents abhorred the four hour crossing to Ostend compared to that of fifty minutes to Calais, (where the Calais-Brussels Pullman provided a connection, should you wish to visit Brussels). Having never stayed in Dover, it was a surprise to learn that every engine in the district, wishing to turn round, visited the *Lord Warden*! Moreover much the easiest way of turning the larger engines, which were based at Stewarts Lane, was to circumnavigate the hotel itself, using the triangle whenever the main line was not occupied by a train, changing direction at Hawkesbury Street and Archcliff Junctions.

In those days railway enthusiasts were few and the *Lord Warden* did not advertise that there were constant engine movements all the time! The 0-6-2 and 0-6-0 tanks sent from Brighton that were allocated to Dover Marine for carriage shunting, along with the inevitable 0-4-4 tanks on local trains, all I believe visited the shed roads for the water crane. The 'R1' 0-6-0 tanks from Folkestone sub-shed occasionally made an appearance for heavy maintenance, while the shed pilot was usually one of the little 'P' class 0-6-0 tanks, such as the one preserved on the 'Bluebell Railway' in Sussex, and now appropriately named *Bluebell*.

With nationalization, of course the Hotel was renamed 'Southern House' and turned into offices. These are still occupied today by Sealink Stena Line. You reached it by a long footbridge over the tracks, from Dover Marine's platforms and this was later extended for the foot passengers using the train ferry. Dover shed is now demolished, so that even if I had realised my idea of retirement as a permanent resident, there would be little to see apart from the pair of Class '33s' that shunt the ferry freight, which have a refuelling point nearby.

But no one imagined such things in 1937, with the 'Night Ferry' running, the Channel Tunnel blocked by Parliament in 1930, and the busy boat trains, for airliners were slow and of course the jet engine had yet to be invented.

The shed was full of 4-4-0s. The 'L1' and 'L' classes, double-headed most boat trains. There were some 'Schools', and I believe a very few 'King Arthurs'. The 'D1s' and 'E1s' also worked on boat trains, but often these were reliefs. Important trains like the *Golden Arrow* had 'Lord Nelsons' and 'King Arthurs' visiting from Stewarts Lane, and sometimes 'Schools' as well.

Another feature of Dover Marine's enormous covered station, with its huge platforms so suitable for marching soldiers in wartime, for it was completed during World War I, and holiday crowds post World War II, was that it was then a through station and the empty trains passed up the Pier to the seaward end, then reversed down lines between the station and the original Pier with its raised walkway used by anglers, out to the sidings beside either the *Lord Warden's* lounge or the smoking room. In addition, the ordinary trains to Canterbury, Maidstone East, Chatham and London, ran empty in and out of the station. Thus there was something going on almost all the time, between the Up departing boat trains and the arriving Down ones, which were often almost simultaneous, as they were for different boats. Coal wagons with coal for the steamers needed shunting, too. Consequently the *Lord Warden* was not full to bursting with holiday makers who occupied the hotels on the sea front. For even when nothing was happening, every twenty minutes a roaring Leyland TD4, its destination blind labelled Marine Station (Lord Warden), I rather think, would disturb all the guests, on East Kent's Dover Town Service, 96, that had only just replaced the trams which had never crossed the main line.

If anyone noticed the railway lines sunk in the road next to the seafront promenade, the hoteliers pretended they were not used. They were rudely disillusioned by the arrival of a 'P' class in the early morning with a long train of coal trucks for the steamers on the Eastern arm. And it was quite a performance, too. Through what looked like half a level crossing, they entered the road near the old Town station. Here there were points whose levers had to be inserted by the shunters, and blocks of wood removed from the point blades. The line led over a swing bridge by the Wellington Dock where SR ships were often laid up to be refitted. There were ropes between the running and guard rails, so that cart wheels would not drop into them. These ropes had to be lifted out, and afterwards replaced. For some crazy reason the line then ran onto the Prince of Wales Pier, which had extremely light rails on it. This was some a half mile long, and was very decrepid and out of use, though there was a small shelter and people could walk on it. The coal trains had to reverse here to proceed along the sea front. As the 'P' class got the worst coal at Dover shed, the best being given to the express engines, they belched black smoke all over the hotels white-painted welcoming front windows!

Owing to proximity of the cliffs, and Dover Castle, garrisoned until very recently and still, I believe, with some military personnel in it, which towers over the scene, this was the only way to reach the Eastern arm. Here cargo ships tied up, and also Townsend ferry for motorists, which forced the SR to start the *Autocarrier*. Cars were still loaded by crane, though when there was a strike, it was discovered they could roll-on and roll-off. That stopped when the cranedrivers went back to work and was, I think only done at Calais. The land reclamation in the Harbour, the raised roadway inside the docks, and the spiral road that goes out to sea in order to reach the main A2 road on the east side of the Castle at the top of the cliffs, have transformed this part of Dover out of all recognition, since World War II.

The boat trains now are called Channel trains because at Dover Western Docks all you find is a fleet of buses to take you to the ship at Eastern Docks. Last time I returned this way even the bus drivers did not know if they were going to Priory or Western Docks. BR does not care, it is preoccupied with the Channel Tunnel, and it is quite outrageous that the Conservative Government did not force the High Speed Line through in time for it, when they spend a fortune each year on new motorways.

On that day in 1937, though, my generation still believed that World War I was the war to end all wars, for that was what we were taught in school, and my father was so carried away by the comfort of the 'Night Ferry', that seeing one of the train ferries in the dock, he took me over to look at it. The ship was called *Twickenham Ferry*; the other two were called *Hampton Ferry* and *Shepperton Ferry*. I feel sure Sir John Elliot, the SR's inventor of Public Relations, thought of these *Thames* crossing names which just happen to be places where the Southern meets the *Thames* and other railways do not. To my father's surprise, we were invited on board. Undoubtedly this was because the *Twickenham Ferry* was run by the French ALA company, who were glad of a tip and took no notice of the careful SR regulations for keeping unauthorised people away. *Le 'Twick'* as it was affectionately known, lasted right through the war and for around thirty years, longer than the other two. I knew nothing about rugby football matches, and the subtle naming of this ship after something which was well known to most Frenchmen was lost on me at the time. Steeped in GWR lore, I only had hazy London General Omnibus type geography as to where any place was. I had seen Twickenham on the 27s and I had been to Hampton Court though only later did I know that Shepperton had famous film studios.

They showed us everything proudly, including the drains for the sleeper toilets; and they were very proud of the way the wagons with bunker coal for the *Twick's* engines, could be run on board and shovelled straight in, instead of being carried on mens' backs in sacks, as on every other coal burning SR steamer. Going over the train ferry was more interesting because we had not only used the service for the first time when going to Switzerland, breaking the journey in Paris, but had visited the 1937 Exhibition, where there was a superb HO scale model of the entire route, from London to Paris.

I shall never forget the pleasure of my parents at seeing the famous blue and gold Wagons-Lits cars roll into Victoria's Platform 2 behind an old '02' 0-6-0, along with a Pullman for supper, which we did not patronize, and in front another for the ordinary SR carriage passengers, who walked on and off the ferry. For my parents with thirty years of crossing the Channel behind them, the concept of the 'Night Ferry' was sheer bliss. Instead of being dumped on a cold wet quay, first at Dover and then later after the crossing at Calais, it was possible to make the journey snug in bed in a Wagon-Lits car. It was also my idea of bliss and never do I think of it more than when being ferried in a bus from Dover Marine to the ships in Eastern Docks.

The 'Night Ferry' model was, really and truly, the most marvellous model railway I have ever set eyes on. In those days there were no electronics, and nothing like the thousands of model train enthusiasts there are today. So, for a start there were no proper models of the 'Night Ferry' sleepers, which had only one end entrance, and an emergency exit through the pantry or the boiler room, at the other, as these were placed one on each side of the gangway leading to the next car. But there was no question that the models on this system were 'F' class, with their short wheelbase and only nine cabins, instead of twelve and two entrances.

The 'Night Ferry' model train ran every half hour in one direction only, that is to say you waited an hour, if you wished to see a repeat performance in the same direction. You could not get close up to it. The two termini were arranged so you saw the distinctive exterior and the overall roof above the platforms from which the 'Night Ferry' would emerge. The English part of the scene showed Sevenoaks, to which electrification had been extended from Orpington only in 1935, so every few minutes an SR Emu electric train would emerge from Victoria, and excite people into thinking it was the 'Night Ferry'. Close to

Sevenoaks, the train disappeared in either a tunnel or behind some model trees, to re-appear from Victoria once more, some minutes later. On the French side, Chantilly Viaduct was faithfully reproduced, while the Gare du Nord, at the far end from London, had its street facade facing the people watching from that end. Inside the two termini it was sufficiently dark not to be able to see what happened to the trains and whilst the model had of course to be compressed, the activities at Dover and Dunkirk were replicated in some detail.

The 'Night Ferry' arrived, and ran into the model Dover Marine. An SR shunting tank appeared, coupled onto the sleeping cars, drew them out to Hawkesbury Street Junction, and propelled them onto the deck of the train ferry. It then drew off again, and repeated the process on the second track. The shunter retired from whence it had come, behind a model house. The dock gate was then lowered, and the link span having been raised, all done electrically without any sign of human effort, the *Twickenham Ferry* set off across the water. Yes the water, this was the *piece de résistance* of the whole model, for the water was real! Moreover it did not stay still. There were waves, the Ferry rolled!

Eventually it arrived at Dunkirk where it rose realistically or fell, in a real working lock! Then it turned round and went astern past a raised swing bridge, into the ferry berth. Here the linkspan was lowered, a Nord tank engine (a 0-8-0 this time, larger than the SR 0-6-0) came over the span, disappeared into the ferry for a brief moment, and emerged with two sleeping cars, it then went over the points to collect the other two. The 'Night Ferry' train then proceeded to the main line through the street, and over the swing bridge in front of the ferry, now lowered. The model Chapelon Pacific was attached at the other end, and it set off through the model of France, to Paris.

In those days, with no electronics, the whole performance was amazing. All that water, but there were no short circuits! Despite the breaks of line, such as at the swing bridge or the link spans and the train deck, there was no hitch, or sticking, even though the ferry tracks moved, with the ship's crossing! The only thing not shown was the attaching of the 'Lord Nelson' class loco to the sleepers. This took place out of sight in Dover Marine while at Victoria the whole train disappeared out of sight from the terminal end of the station tracks. A similar arrangement took place in the model of Paris. Public and model enthusiasts alike were captivated by the ferry which appeared to have no visible guidance, yet turned round (as of course it had to do at Dover, coming from France), before running into the ferry dock, backwards. The early train ferries were only stern loading.

After the Exhibition was over, the English piece of the model was, I believe, on show at Victoria for a period. But then World War II disrupted the real ferry and after it, the model had vanished. Nobody knew what had happened to it. But what was more extraordinary, nobody knew who made it, and nobody believed it used real water and locks and waves and carriages running on and off the ferry, apart from those who had seen it!

Fifty years went by and in 1987 one last appeal was made in *La Vie du Rail* about it, as nobody had come forward to say who had built it. But this time, an old man over eighty years old, set the record straight. The 'Night Ferry' was not started by French or British Railways: neither existed in 1936, but by 1937, the Nord Railway knew it was due to be nationalized at the end of the year. The Nord was proud of its achievement and thus wanted the model as realistic as possible, and as cheap as possible. It was built by the Nord's engineering apprentices, in their own workshops. The rolling stock, mostly made of lead, was heavy so as not to tip over at bumps in the track where there were moveable joins. The outline was realistic, but all were solid, the details etched on them. The water was realistic enough, thick and dirty in the docks, and fairly deep on the Channel to accommodate the waves. As a result it was totally impossible to see the ferry's keel, and the way it was controlled from underneath. I do not know how the water was prevented from leaking down below. I do know everything was done with magnets, which drew coaches together, and pulled them along, or alternatively uncoupled them when the magnetic pole was changed. As far as I am aware the running rails were not used for any electric purpose, consequently items like the realistic opening swing bridge, and the linkspans could be negiotiated. I do not fully understand how it was done, even now.

Hotel guests were never matey as now. The permanent resident who was given much attention and whose demeanour betrayed 'Retired Colonel' unmistakably (there were no less than eleven of these in our village) glanced out of the window during dinner far less frequently than I, where a 'U' class Mogul was on the turntable. He behaved just like other retired Colonels, who believed youths should not speak until spoken to, and there was nothing to suggest that this one collected steam engines, like other people collected statues and similar works of art. Nor did he. But the famous Colonel H. F. Stephens, whose home was at Tonbridge, rented rooms at Dover in the *Lord Warden*, and he finally died in the hotel, mercifully for him as it turned out, on 23rd October 1931. Fifteen of his engines lived in a shed on the Shropshire and Montgomeryshire railway where just one was needed to run the local traffic. He often wrote telegrams, or his dutiful Manager, a Mr Austen, would come to the *Lord Warden* for luncheon, in the course of visiting the East Kent Railway at nearby Shepherds Well.

My knowledge of Colonel Stephens' railways was nil. All I knew derived from the very first of the *Oakwood Press* paperbacks, with masterful but tiny line drawings by Rodger Kidner, whose moving text really galvanised the rail enthusiast movement. But don't knock the Southern, for their attitude to Colonel Stephens was in many respects benign, I feel. After all, they took the 0-8-0 tank *Hecate* off him, as it was too heavy for his wobbly tracks, but did they really want it?

They did not pay him for it, but exchanged it for a worn-out ex-LSWR 0-6-0 Saddle Tank of Beattie's '330' class, which they had already withdrawn for scrapping. It gave nothing but trouble, while the SR got a bargain in *Hecate* although Maunsell had decided that his own 0-8-0 'Z' class Tanks should be superseded by diesel shunters. So perhaps the SR were not so benign, after all. I feel sure the 0-8-0T were inspired by 0-8-0T on the Nord – why not have 0-6-0Ts like everybody else, otherwise? The diesel-electrics would give great savings in preparation and disposal time, and operation by one man instead of two.

Colonel Stephens, like everybody of his generation, was unaware until too late, of the motor revolution. Before I was born, lorries were massive things on solid tyres, often steam driven or consuming petrol at an unremunerative rate, even at one shilling and sixpence per gallon (10 litres – 7½p). It was the wages explosion after World War I which changed the railways, as with everything else. The Colonel declined to join his railways to the proposed Southern. Some minor railways which escaped the grouping seemed viable to the Colonel, if run on the cheap. And he did not ignore the motorbus. He got Model T Fords and ran them back to back with rail wheels, on the Hundred of Manhood or West Sussex Railway, from Chichester to Selsey Bill; and on some other lines. What totally flummoxed many people in the late 1920s was the realisation that buses had become speedy, reliable and comfortable, with the advent of Mr Rackham's Leyland Titan TD1 and the AEC Regent, and the heavy duty pneumatic tyre. The railways were still horse and cart orientated. Any vision of London street traffic up until about 1951 is incomplete without blockages caused by an LMS horse and cart: The GW & SR and LNER had been less backward in getting motor vehicles, particularly the Scammell three-ton and six-ton three wheeled, easily manoeuvreable Mechanical Horse. Ever thought why it had this old-fashioned name? Not tractor, or tug? To get railways to buy it.

After our night in the *Lord Warden*, the next morning we had to have a taxi to Dover Priory station. The train, when it came, had I think a 'U' class Mogul, but it could have been an 'N'. The carriages were the comfortable chocolate and cream variety, not by any means the newest, but adequate. I looked forward to luncheon in the dining car or in the compartment, only to discover that luncheon was not served until after Reading. Travelling through the tunnel, round the curve under the very bridge that the taxi had used, in a Great Western carriage seemed very curious indeed. Just to get started took the best part of an hour, before the *Lord Warden* was finally out of sight, a typically Southern start, I thought, to an interminable journey to Reading, taking nearly five hours altogether. A Dover-London boat train took about two hours, London-Reading a mere hour at most and if one allowed perhaps an hour to reach Paddington from Victoria, the wisdom of going home cross country in this train, could be called into question.

Not for us the sixty miles an hour, non-stop run from Dover to Tonbridge. We called at Folkestone Central, Shorncliffe Camp, Ashford and Tonbridge, and this time, peering out as we ran leisurely through Headcorn, there was no sign of life whatever on the Colonel's Kent and East Sussex Railway. A large chunk of this line is preserved from Tenterden Town to Northiam and eventually it may link up with the SR's '1066' Tonbridge-Hastings line at Robertsbridge. The K&ESR's *Wealden Pullman* has run for fifteen years, with splendid Pullman-style dinners and a bar in Pullman Car *Barbara*. On the *Wealden Pullman* you will find golden croutons as inseparable from the soup as they once were aboard the *Golden Arrow*. There is also excellent English white wine, produced at Tenterden, served on board.

After Tonbridge, the formidable run, – which I have never made since – by Penshurst, Edenbridge, Godstone and Nutfield: and I think we stopped at all of them, omitting only Lyghe Halt. A few miles beyond Edenbridge came Crowhurst East Junction where a spur joined the Oxted and East Grinstead line. Then after Nutfield, the line swung north over the top of Quarry tunnel, into Redhill station, out of sight of the Quarry line by which Brighton Expresses missed out Redhill.

Tonbridge-Redhill has had to wait until 1992 and the completion of the Channel Tunnel to get electrified, which just shows the dominance of London. The original South Eastern main line to Dover, miles round out of the direct way, it ought to have been wired on 25kV as a start to joining the AC overhead at the Tunnel with the West Coast and East Coast main lines north of London to be used by the dual voltage Class '92' freight engines. But as the commuters are far more important than Tunnel traffic, it is to be third rail DC as in 1925, with a few technical improvements. Whether Redhill to Reading will ever be properly electrified is anybody's guess. Redhill-Reigate was electrified in 1932, but the portions of line from Guildford to Ash, and Wokingham to Reading were being made ready only in 1937, and opened the following year.

Under the joint working arrangements between the GWR and the SR, SR Moguls as mentioned, ran on from Reading to Oxford, and GWR Moguls could go from Reading to Redhill. Folklore has it that a GWR Mogul was once stopped at Redhill for being out of gauge. The train of course called at Reigate. After the leisurely Redhill reversal, it ambled across Surrey, stopping certainly at Dorking Town and Shalford, and I think at Betchworth, Deepdene, Gomshall & Shere, and Chilworth & Albury as well. Then round onto the Up Portsmouth-London main line, newly electrified and making us wait at Shalford Junction, before setting into Guildford. Another pause here for water, as at most places along the route. Then over all the complicated junctions, left to Wanborough, right at Ash Junction, stop at Ash, for Aldershot.

There was not another reversal at Guildford, for the line was always intended to be a through route to Reading. I believe, Prince Albert took a personal interest in this line, almost straight, leading from the Army's large establishment at Aldershot, to those at Shorncliffe and Dover Castle to enable troops to be embarked for Europe. Here the grimmest part of the line begins, as suburban Surrey, smiling whenever not built over, gives way to Hampshire, county of millionaires and military. We bore right at Aldershot South Junction, and dived under the Alton-Farnham-Aldershot-Ash Vale-Pirbright Junction line (see Chapter Seven), with its nice new electric trains that reduced the Meon Valley line to mere push-pull auto trains with 'M7' 0-4-4Ts, finally ousting the 'A12 Jubilees', to gloomy North Camp with its rudimentary shelters. On under the SR main line from Waterloo to Basingstoke and Southampton and the West of England to yet another stop this time at Farnborough North. Then Blackwater, Sandhurst Halt, but after diving beneath the main A30 road to the west at a bridge that for years was a motorists' death trap, the line takes on a different hue, entering Royal Berkshire, and after Crowthorne is Wokingham. Here the line is joined by the former LSWR 's London-Reading line, so for the rest of the way the train pretended to be an Express. Winnersh, Woodley and Earley were passed non-stop, and for a brief moment the line took on familiarity. The train shot over the bridge across the main A4 Newbury-Reading-London, actually known as the Bath Road (from the days when the Beaux of London visited Bath) which formed the Borough boundary and the terminus of Reading Corporation's trams. To the right were Sutton's Seeds trial grounds, now long gone, which separated the SR from the GW. At this point the Restaurant Car Conductor came along the train announcing luncheon. Sweeping past some gasometers, the Great Western was on the right, but not of course connected there until during the war. Our train slowed down as it descended to ground level and the junction just outside Reading's SR terminus, long removed now, to climb up the steep bank, used now by the Waterloo electrics, and mentioned in *Gone with Regret*, to leave the seductive Southern past a GW signal board still marked 'To SE&C' in 1937, and arrive in Reading's Down main platform 1. The train now looked like any other Great Western one: and it was time for us to alight.

Perhaps one should not knock the Southern, but memories of that never ending journey caused us to motor to Dover, on future trips. BR now runs diesel railcars to Gatwick from Reading. But nothing to Dover. Close your eyes slightly and a vision may appear of Mr Stirling's stately 'F' class 4-4-0s with those enormous wheels. They rather dwarfed Mr Drummond's machines with similar wheel arrangement that I recall but dimly on London trains, for electrification arrived in 1938, the third rail diverging at Wokingham. But don't knock the Southern, for this line came into its own in 1940 during the epic of Dunkirk, though it is ironic that Prince Albert's vision of a line to put British troops onto the continent, should have proved so useful in rescuing the survivors of our defeated armies.

Chapter Ten

Southampton Docks

That eminent SR railway man, John Rogers (later I believe, a prominent teacher at BR's Woking Staff College), whom I knew slightly when at Cambridge during my Oxford days, later told me that the people who operated the London West Control had a terrible time with Southampton Docks. Once an engine had disappeared inside, it did not come out again! No amount of agitating the Docks Department could get it to emerge, however desperately it might be needed, somewhere else! I could not imagine such a thing happening in the many GWR Docks where everybody was madly loyal to the Great Western, not just their little bit of it. Only GW critics maintained everything was exactly the same throughout the system. For instance the GWR dock engines in Swansea were neither GW-built nor wholly GW designed, but built by Avonside in Bristol.

But one look at the all black dock engines in Southampton would show the close relationship of those funny little 0-4-0Ts which were LSWR Class 'B4', and Mr Adams 'A12' 'Jubilees'. After all, he designed both and superintended their building, though some 'Jubilees' were built by outside contractors in Scotland. But here the distinction ended. For the dock engines apparently did not belong to the Southern! They did not have 'SOUTHERN' on them. Black instead of green, they had brass nameplates instead of large numbers (these were small, near the cab), and their names were mostly French, exactly like their whistles! One was said to have had its motion sealed by Customs, when the driver was caught smuggling! Nobody seems to have mentioned this, for they did not go to France, like me, in 1929, before being introduced to Southampton Docks in 1932, on the *Olympic*, the sister ship of the ill-fated *Titanic*. At any rate it had four funnels, and a great number of decks. Viewed from the boat deck, it towered over the sheds, and I recall that all mention of the *Titanic* was taboo.

The RMS *Olympic*, to give this Steamer her proper title, was not, in fact, the White Star Line's flagship. This was the *Majestic*, a ship delivered new as part of Germany's war reparations. The crew wore proper sailor suits with White Star or RMS *Olympic* hatbands and all mention of Cunard was as taboo as the *Titanic*. Due to the slump, Cunard had just taken over their arch rival, which was extremely confusing, since the ship was now 'Cunard White Star', 'not the same as Cunard', just as the dock engines, apparently, were 'not really Southern'.

There were a dozen of them. Where they got their little trucks from, and what they were doing with them, was one mystery. How they did not crash into each other was another. Most of them had hardly any cabs, which did not matter that boiling hot August day when I first saw them, and the cut away cabs gave more room for shunters. It was also easier to get at the coal, for just like French tank engines, the 'B4s' had no bunkers.

Do not imagine there were no *real* SR engines in the docks. Of course there were, arriving on the boat trains and on the freight trains, and departing on goods trains full of imports, from the main marshalling sidings near the Old Docks main gate; but while most tanks were 0-6-0, I was fascinated by the 0-4-0Ts which were just like my Hornby gauge 'O' engines. The vast majority of the dock railway was laid in road-ways, with guard rails, and the squealing of the flanges mingled with the piercing shrieks of the whistles directed at the various lorries and cars, of which there were many.

The New Docks, opened in 1932, were already nearly built. We sailed from the Old Docks. But the system of taking the boat trains away into the road, and down the street past the end of Royal Pier, eventually to the new six road carriage sidings housing seventy-two coaches in the New Docks where a large carriage shed had been built, could all be seen from the *Olympic*, though boat trains for other liners could not, except at a distance.

The deck was almost empty as the passengers were busy settling into their cabins for the week's voyage to New York. But as we were going no further than Cherbourg, we had no cabin. My father was busy saving money again. He could not see why we could not remain on deck, or in one of the saloons if it was wet. White Star were quite horrified by this, as all passengers were allocated their cabin steward to more or less look after them on the voyage.

I believe there must have been some deck stewards, too, but their duties did not include mollycoddling cross-Channel passengers. But because of this my father set off early in the car with his party, for the thirty mile drive to Southampton. Already the notion of travelling on the Didcot, Newbury and Southampton line had become obsolete, for first we would have had to drive to Highclere Station and then get a taxi from Southampton Terminus. In passing, it often seems to me the railways have never emerged from the horse and cart era, where the powerful, wonderfully fast steam train must have first consideration, and passengers, having to put themselves out to use it, were of no importance. At the slightest whim, today, you are bundled into a bus rather than persuade the train to go alongside the steamer, as of yore – at least for boat trains from capital cities.

Southampton Docks layout always struck me as rather strange. For a start, one of the sharpest curves in the Old Docks had to be traversed to get into the engine shed or Motive Power Depot as modern people like to call it, using three words instead of two, and then using an acronym MPD. This arrangement made sure that no *proper Southern* engines could possibly use it, or the water crane. This was perfectly satisfactory when all the boat trains were planned, 'B4s' were in abundance to take care of the shunting, and all a main line engine had to do was hook off, run round, and be escorted out of the docks by a shunter who operated the mystery telephones which prevented the 'B4s' from colliding with each other or any other engines in the docks.

Engines required to haul freight trains out of the docks, or take boat trains up to London, were timed to arrive light engine, to make their way to the various platforms where boat trains waited for their disembarking passengers. But when economies set in, and fifteen of the 0-6-0 tanks sent by the US Army for shunting military trains all over Europe, were bought to replace the 'B4s', their short wheel base and general light weight, making them ideal, main line engines were needed to do considerably more, or were kept waiting on freight trains for sometimes astonishingly long periods before release and there was even the danger that they might run out of water! Water was of course available just outside the Old Docks for these engines, at Southampton Terminus. So precious Old Docks space was not given over to water cranes, or engine roads, although there were reception and departure sidings. Most passenger liners only carried limited cargo, delivered or received from vans, placed alongside by the 'B4s'.

Many readers will wonder what the fifteenth USA tank was, for it never carried its number 30075 but was cannibalised as spare parts for the others. However, its number has been carefully revived by the Swanage Railway who have imported another USA/TC tank, from Yugoslav Railways which will carry the number 30075.

For many years Mr Reginald Biddle presided over the docks. Mr Biddle was a Jerseyman, and Jerseymen are known for their business acumen and proud independence. The fact that SR controllers might need an engine urgently to do something else outside the docks, was nothing to do with *him*.

Another feature of the layout was that the main railway entrance was separate to the main gate (it still is). The gates were opened and the gateman with flag and handbell walked into the middle of Canute Road outside, and stopped the traffic until 1981 when flashing lights were installed, while the railway crossing keeper performed the same duty on the other side of the train admitted to, or received from the docks, onto the lines adjoining Southampton Terminus. From here there is a straight run up the line to London which at Northam meets the main line from Bournemouth and the New Docks. This was until 1966 a triangular junction, the bottom half being used mostly by trains from Romsey and Andover which had usually come off the GW's former Midland and South Western Junction line from Swindon and Cheltenham, to work into Southampton Terminus. To this day there is a speed restriction on the mainline curve that joins the Bournemouth line to the main Southampton Terminus-Eastleigh line, although everything goes that way now and Southampton Central handles all the city's traffic, Southampton Terminus having been closed as long ago as 1966.

In steam days I believe, the triangle was used by engines wishing to turn, that is those which were too long for the Terminus turntable, though light engine running, tender-first, to and from Eastleigh, the SR's only Southampton shed besides the docks one, was commonplace. It is, after all, not much more than five miles to Eastleigh, where the running shed had the back up of the railway works. The boat trains mostly had regular paths, the Liners leaving at the same time of day, once a week. Arrivals were another matter. No radar, of course and fog in Southampton Water could easily delay them.

Facing south, the Old Docks are bounded by the *River Itchen* on the left or east and the *Test* on the west. On the west side, basins were made for Liners to tie up, including from 1936, the *Queen Mary*. There were two small basins on the *Itchen*, the one furthest up river called the Outer Dock was exclusively used by the Southern's own ships to Le Havre, St. Malo, Guernsey and Jersey. There was one Channel Islands ship on weekdays, and two at weekends. The other basin, the Empress Dock but invariably called Berth 23, was used by the SR's cargo boats to these places.

The docks engine shed was in the vicinity of the Outer Dock, and this area had its own road approach, Gate No.5, and originally two entrances for trains, parallel to each other curving off to the east, that is a left hand bend when seen looking down the tracks past Southampton Terminus. They crossed Canute Road at right angles. The main double track entrance to the docks through Gate 3 is now the only one left. This main line bears right across Canute Road. Inside the docks, a line more or less parallel to Canute Road, linked the two areas. This was essentially to allow the dock engines to reach their shed when they were working in the reception sidings and the Liner berths.

Just inside Gate 3, another line led off from the entrance tracks bearing right and led out of the docks onto the line running along the Town Quay to the Royal Pier. A further line led directly to this one from the reception sidings, forming a triangle. The lines here did not belong to the SR but to the Southampton Harbour Commissioners. Originally there was a station on the Royal Pier and the whole was connected by a tramway leaving the railway at its exit onto Canute Road opposite Dock Gate No.3, and running along Canute Road, which also had the Corporation electric trams on parallel tracks to it, running down Canute Road to the floating bridge across the *Itchen*. A large new bridge, spanning the main line and goods lines between Northam and Southampton Terminus, enabled the trams to be moved from Canute Road in 1882, and the train tramway was also removed, though the part in front of the dock main offices was used as sidings.

Shunting on the Town Quay and Royal Pier, used by the Isle of Wight steamers which have no Customs restrictions, was carried out from about 1922 or earlier until 1957 by two small Drummond 'C14' class 0-4-0Ts, lighter and with a wheelbase even shorter than the 'B4s'. These were SR Nos. 3741 & 3744, renumbered 30588 and 30589 by BR. A sister engine 0745, which was renumbered 77s in 1927, was used in Redbridge sleeper depot. Here one engine was kept permanently, in its own shed. Vast numbers of sleepers were imported by way of Redbridge Wharf, on the *Test* where the tidal area ends, and the main line to Bournemouth crosses the *Test*, after passing Southampton Central, Millbrook and Redbridge Stations. Sleepers were creosoted on narrow gauge trolleys. The 'C14s' were originally built for working steam rail cars, and as such had single drivers for which Drummond had a great fondness. This did not stop him converting them to 0-4-0Ts when they were detached from their carriage portions. No.77s replaced the former inmate of the LSWR's Permanent Way Works, a 0-6-0ST of Adams 'G6' class, in 1927. The works carried out rail welding latterly, and the whole site was closed down in 1989.

I passed along here in 1959, for the first time, having occasion to see someone in Bournemouth, when I thought I could see him in Southampton. So by total chance I found I was able to catch the 'Bournemouth Belle', with only a short time to wait. I decided I could afford First Class for the thirty-five miles plus a much lower supplement than going all the way from London. This was quite the most sumptuous Pullman journey I have ever made, for I was ushered into *Topaz*, just a few weeks before its chairs were seized for the 1960s-built Metropolitan-Cammell Pullmans with BR type bodyshells, then under construction. *Topaz* was rescued for posterity by Mr Henry Maxwell, who bought the car and presented it to what is now the National Railway Museum, and all can see the superb marquetry and panelling in this car of March 1914, the work of the craftsmen of the Birmingham Railway Carriage and Wagon Company. Moreover I made my only visit to Bournemouth West in it, a terminus now torn up, like the Somerset & Dorset Joint Railway, whose LMS style trains were its principal users.

At the Millbrook-Redbridge end of the New Docks, the SR built an enormous new graving dock, capable of dry-docking the *Queen Mary*, which was named the King George V Dock by His Majesty when he opened it in 1933. The floor is of 25 ft thick concrete. It is 1200 ft long, 135 ft wide and 45 ft deep. Sir Herbert Walker did things on the grand scale, and like the graving dock, the New Docks were enormous. A quay wall was built along the east bank of the *Test*, and over 400 acres of mud behind it was re-claimed, using chalk from the large chalk pit dug out behind Micheldever station. Previously the main line from Southampton to Millbrook passed close to the water's edge.

Eight berths were constructed and each was provided with a shed 900 ft long and 150 ft wide, which could accommodate one of the four funnelled liners then usually at work for the various steamship lines. These lines were then household names: Cunard, United States Lines, Royal Mail Steam Packet Company, Union Castle (every Thursday to South Africa), Blue Star Line, and not forgetting White Star, just taken over by Cunard. The quay wall was 7,400 ft long. Inside each shed was a large circulating area for Customs examination, and on the landward side there was a platform for the boat trains. There were crossovers between each shed and a running line at the back of them, next to the road, which is called Herbert Walker Avenue, that runs along throughout. Each shed could be serviced independently and the train engines could take the empty boat trains to the new carriage shed and sidings already mentioned. From 1932-35 all trains into the New Docks had to use the single extension to the sidings on the Town Quay. This meant that they ran along the street for part of the way, in front of the landward end of the Royal Pier, whether they were full or empty, hauled by Express engines, over the Harbour Board's line to the Old Docks and the Canute Road entrance to the Southern Railway beside Southampton Terminus. But when I sailed in the *Olympic*, only the sidings and carriage shed were in use. The first ship to use the New Docks was berthed in December 1932.

Before the carriage shed came into use, boat train coach sets had to be stabled at Eastleigh, near Northam, on sidings between Walton and Weybridge, and at Clapham, along with the trains that serviced Waterloo. So I believe that many of these myriad trains seen processing through Micheldever, and later from the Winchester playing field, in fact were empty!

The new carriage shed faced towards the Royal Pier end of the layout, so that dock engines arriving to take an empty boat train to the Old Docks, could run straight in. As the New Docks quayside sheds had entrances at either end, the arriving boat trains engines could run right through, with the coaches stopped at the platform and the engine, or at least its chimney, outside. At the Millbrook end of the New Docks, there were six tracks on the main line as far as Central. The four on the right looking down the line from the Central Station were used by ordinary trains to and from Bournemouth or Romsey, which line diverges after Redbridge Station, leading to Andover and the Midland & South Western line, eventually. The GWR had running powers over this, inherited from the MSWJ, and GW engines worked into the docks regularly for the 7.34 pm goods to Cheltenham, from the Old Docks reception sidings.

The two tracks on the left led round a 'U' turn to enter the New Docks from the Millbrook end. Engines waiting to get through Southampton to run light engine to Eastleigh, did not impede either the docks or the main line. But engines bringing a boat train, which were based at Nine Elms (London), often needed to return on another, Up boat train, serving of course a different Liner, quite quickly. So a seventy foot turntable was installed, and also facilities for watering engines, at the entrance to the docks from the Millbrook end. The New Docks made things easier for Liners to come alongside and ships of companies like French Line would call for a few hours only. Something altogether better was planned for Cunard. The *Queen Mary* was too big to occupy just one berth, anyway, so plans were made for an Ocean Terminal at the Royal Pier end of the New Docks, which were eventually realised in 1950. Relations with Cunard had always been close and cordial, and it is not generally known that the SR ran a Travel Bureau on board the *Queen Mary* from her maiden voyage up to the start of World War II in 1939. The Travel Bureau in the Cabin Class Reception area of the RMS *Queen Mary* was staffed and run by the SR, and also served the three other railway companies. Open in the mornings, Tourist and Third Class passengers were served from a table in their lounges in the afternoons with a hang-up 'SR Travel Bureau' notice board. Five Ocean Liner boat trains were needed to clear the ship, and printed tickets with reservations for these were issued by staff, often working all night on the last leg of the fourteen day return voyage. A similar complimentary service was provided for US railroads and airlines for ship's passengers, their representatives boarding on arrival to collect the details. The bureau issued hand written paper tickets to all destinations of the other British railway companies, if required, as well as providing tourist information and railway hotel bookings. When the ship was delayed by bad weather, and the Master decided to put into Plymouth, the bureau staff of two, had to telegraph to the GWR and arrange for their boat trains (including the Ocean Saloons) to be provided. Sometimes when this had all been done the Master found he could reach Southampton after all and the hastily arranged GWR trains had to be cancelled. Paths for boat trains were planned at various times of day, for use when necessary. Cabin Class corresponded to First Class today. The service suspended on outbreak of War, in September 1939, and was never resumed, nor ever implemented on board the *Queen Elizabeth*, though this was planned. The picture of the bureau has been provided by Mr N. E. Norman who was actually the trainee earmarked to run the bureau on the *Queen Elizabeth*. The trainee also acted as a relief for the two SR staff continuously on board.

All this lasted about seven years. Then came the war, and altogether about four million troops passed through the docks. Southampton was also badly blitzed. The rapid development of air travel in the last two decades makes it easy to forget that Liner traffic was still very heavy in the 1950s, with over 1000 boat trains per annum in each direction, and nearly 6000 freight trains. Total track mileage of both docks was seventy-seven, which was almost the distance from Waterloo to Southampton.

Stabling the boat trains at Southampton instead of Clapham gave Pullman staff some headaches. They were expected to draw their stores from the Battersea Depot, and load them into the 'Bournemouth Belle's' brake van. That was the easy bit, the 'Belle' stabling at Stewarts Lane which adjoined the depot. On arrival at Southampton in it, they had to hire a taxi, move everything into the 'Cunarder' and then sleep the night on the floors of the unheated cars, to be ready for the excursion down the street to the Old Docks, after the New Docks Ocean Terminal had been given up (it is now pulled down), ready for an early Up morning departure. The Pullman was always the first train to leave after the ship started discharging passengers, and the last to leave Waterloo, to arrive just prior to the ship sailing. The Pullmans served the *Queen Mary*, *Queen Elizabeth*, and with a change of roofboard, the rival *United States*, the Blue Riband holder, until taken in June 1990 by 'SeaCat' Hoverspeed *Great Britain*. Single Pullmans ran in some of the other boat trains, too.

Problems with strikes, hastened the downfall of Southampton Docks. This happened anyway at a time when people were begining to take to the air in greater numbers. To make matters worse, the British Transport Commission divorced the Southern Region of its Railway Executive from the former SR owned and run docks, handing them to the Docks & Inland Waterways Executive, causing the difficulties mentioned at the beginning of the Chapter. In the 1930s on August Bank Holiday weekend there could be over twenty ships arriving or leaving, served by up to forty boat trains. Main line steam survived on the Bournemouth line until 1966-7. In 1962, the Transport Act severed the docks from the railway. BR ordered Class '03' and Class '14' diesel shunters to replace steam in the docks. The USA tanks had been supplemented by ex LBSC 0-6-0Ts ('E1' class). The decline of the docks rail traffic and lines was gradual. The Docks shed ceased to be used in 1966, the Harbour Board line into the New Docks was closed in 1979.

By 1992, Associated British Ports, who took over Southampton when docks were privatised, had raised their charges so greatly for any trains using their dock lines, that BR InterCity, who had taken over the single boat train that sufficed for the *Queen Elizabeth 2*, found in 1992 they could no longer run the train. Cunard anyway charged its passengers extra to use it, while providing free tickets, included in the passage money (as sea fares are properly called) to Southampton Central from anywhere in Britain. The Pullman Car Company was finally nationalized in 1962, and no time was lost in removing all Ocean Liner Pullmans, in 1963. After the electrification of the Bournemouth line, some of the '71' class BB electric engines built at Doncaster were rebuilt as Class '74' electro-diesels, for working the Ocean Liner boat trains. They also worked the 'Night Ferry'. But Southern Region has always detested loco-hauled trains. They disliked the '74s' because they were built at Doncaster, while the '73s', built at Eastleigh as electro-diesels for the Hastings line, still non electric at the time, were preferred, and have survived to operate the InterCity Gatwick Expresses, and Royal Specials to the Derby. Miraculously since 1982, they have been available for the 'Venice-Simplon-Orient Express', and to the end, they worked boat trains for the *QE 2*, which ran to the *QE 2*'s berth at the extreme end of the Old Docks Peninsular, Berth 38. Very often the SR preferred to run Class '33s', wastefully using diesels over the third rail all the way from Waterloo to Southampton.

No description of Southampton would be complete without mentioning the SR Steamers. Maybe this chapter should have been called 'Ships I have nearly been sick on'. Whereas Dover and Folkestone attracted the glamour, since those routes are the shortest, Southampton carried about a third of the total number of passengers using the SR ships at those two ports and many more than went by Newhaven. The SR's Continental services to Le Havre and St. Malo only ran three days a week in winter. But, according to Sir John Elliott, the SR's Preferred and Ordinary dividend was all paid for out of profits from the Continental traffic. The SR continued the practice of the pre-grouping companies by charging on the boat trains, fares that were higher than the ordinary fares, between London and the Channel Ports.

With some exceptions Southern ships were nearly all built by Denny Brothers of Dumbarton in Scotland. The train ferries, like the *Twickenham Ferry*, which we have already met, were built on the *Tyne* by Swan, Hunter. In 1936 there were nineteen passenger ships, and a dozen cargo vessels, not counting the three jointly owned passenger and three cargo ships flying the French flag on the Newhaven-Dieppe run, whose ships were the fastest on the Channel at one time, cruising at 24 knots. The service had been Anglo-French since about 1852 until 1984, when the *Senlac* was sold by Sea Containers to the French. She carried the LBSCR house flag, a red cross on white background up to the end, over sixty years after the end of the LBSCR.

Considering all the difficulties facing the Southern in the 1920s, the Company did much to modernise their fleet. The *Dinard* and the *St Briac* arrived new from Denny's in 1924 for the Southampton-St. Malo service. The size of the vessels was governed by the lock at St. Malo's harbour entrance, where the enormous tides have a forty feet drop on some days.

A dam across the *River Rance*, linking St. Malo to Dinard by road and saving fifteen miles, makes use of these tides. This dam generates hydro-electricity with turbines driven by the tide in both directions. Instead of nasty huge muddy banks at low tide, the river has water all the time and is now extremely beautiful. The *Rance* is tidal up to Dinant, and expresses from Paris ran from both St. Malo, and Dinard via Dinant, until the 1980s when the Dinard line closed. It latterly ran only in summer. Now Paris-Rennes has TGV trains, passengers mostly have to change there to diesel autorails.

In 1938, my father decided to motor in France, taking me with him, overnight uneventfully in the *Hantonia*. A journey passing innumerable steam tramways, or tortillards that I was never permitted to stop and explore. First we had to race to Flers to meet my mother, who had left us at Le Havre to visit friends in Paris for the day. Then we had to rush on to Brittany where my father had booked the hotel rooms, and was in no mood to delay, for fear of night driving. By the time I returned to France post war, these little lines were no more.

We returned on the *St Briac*. By then the war scare was on and passengers with cars, desperate to get to Britain, were being advised to go via Hamburg, since the ship was full. A few went to Jersey and changed ships there. With no radar, we arrived in dense fog up the *Solent* and *Southampton Water*, where the siren of a departing Liner we never saw, hooted at us with ever louder menace. The *St Briac's* master kept to his side of the water so close inshore, that he inadvertently turned slightly into the *River Hamble* and ran aground. Thereupon he refused to budge until noon, when the sun at last broke through on this early September day, and he backed off unassisted. However there was no food. The SR gave the ships just enough for the return passage, and that should have ended at breakfast time.

This was my first introduction to the basin called the Outer Dock, off the *Itchen*, with its fixed buoy in the centre, to which ships attached a bow wire, enabling them to pull out past the ship tied up next in front, and also turn, or swing as it is called. Though the whole business seemed ridiculously small, like the ships, and rather old fashioned, the size of Channel Islands vessels was governed by the miniscule entrance to Jersey's St. Helier Harbour. A new harbour here was finally opened by the Duke of Normandy, named *Elizabeth Harbour* after her, in 1988-9. By this time BR had been forced to sell Sealink in 1984, and its new owner, Sea Containers, withdrew from the Channel Islands in 1987, after spending millions refitting the two ships *Earl Granville* and *Earl Godwin* which ran the service from 1977 or so onward.

The Southern bought three new ships for the Channel Islands service in 1930-1, in spite of the slump. The first *Isle of Jersey*, seemed the best of the bunch. Her Jersey Master on one occasion when there was a peak high tide, saved twenty minutes after departing late from Southampton due to boat train delays, by taking her inside Corbiére Lighthouse at the South Western point of the Island, which you would hardly believe, should you visit the Island and go and look. Captain Le Breuilly was very good seaman, but I never travelled with him. The *Isle of Guernsey* was also a stalwart, available whenever either of the other two were out of service, and also used as a relief ship especially on Saturdays when separate ships sailed from Southampton to Guernsey and Jersey, one to each Island. My voyages on her were rare. They were all sister ships.

The ship the Southern liked the best (and all were, of course, built by

Denny of Dumbarton) was the most modern, the *Isle of Sark*. They were very proud of the Denny-Brown stabilizers fitted in her. These had never been put in a vessel before, and consisted of plates which stuck out from the ship's sides at sea and operated contrary to the waves, endeavouring to lessen the upheaval. Unlike their successors which often gave up reaching Jersey when the weather was foul, sheltering in St Peter Port, Guernsey instead, the *Isle of Sark* sailed whatever the weather, and the passengers suffered considerably. The Southern were excited by the stabilizers. They were fitted at the request of Dennys to try them out. Considered successful, larger versions were installed in the *Queen Mary* after World War II. I always steadfastly maintained that this anti-rolling device enabled the *Sark*, in which I had the misfortune to voyage quite often, to roll considerably all the time, even in calm weather. This was strenuously denied by all Southern officials as untrue. They claimed the rolling was due to the 'Maier-type' bow. However, don't knock the Southern, because those same officials admitted, after the *Isle of Sark* was withdrawn in favour of the *Caesarea* and *Sarnia*, new in 1961, that of course this was the case!

The Islands are part of the Duchy of Normandy, whose Duke William in 1066, conquered England. Owing to the nasty seas between the Islands and the rest of the Duchy, the Dukes appointed Bailiffs to look after their interests. To this day the President of the States (Etats) as the Island Parliaments are called, and of the Royal Court, is known as the Bailiff, the Guernsey Bailiwick extending to all the smaller Islands, though they have their own administrations. The Islands have their own money, postage stamps, police, and low income tax (20% for residents) due to King John, having lost the rest of his Duchy, giving the Islands independence in 1201. The present Duke is Her Majesty the Queen, and the Islands are Crown property, and though never part of the United Kingdom, they were part of the Southern. Jersey Station and Guernsey Stations were marked by standard green SR metal boards so visitors would not get off at the wrong Island for their holidays! The gangways had Jersey or Guernsey painted on them, just like Dover or Folkestone.

In the 1930s slump, the GWR and Southern Railways arranged a joint service, running in winter three days a week each from Southampton or Weymouth. The Southern looked after Jersey and had its own berth at the Albert Quay, used as the passenger port until 1989's new harbour, and SR lorries, locally registered with Southern & Great Western on them, provided the cartage. The GWR used the New North Quay. In Guernsey the ships shared the quay, where they rarely stopped for long, and the GWR ran the locally registered lorries, lettered GW&SR, like the Upwey-Portland bus, the SR's only bus route from 1923-1934, jointly run by the GWR with vehicles hired from Southern National in 1933-4.

Armed with a ticket written out by hand, a single 'Highclere to Jersey via Cheesehill' which GW fans would know meant Winchester, and also that by 1956 it was spelt Chesil correctly – Highclere's foreman was 100 per cent GWR – I left my home for ever. It seemed romantic enough at the time, though actually I returned for nearly a year. A porter took our belongings from the Southampton Terminus to Canute Road. There a docks porter had to be summoned. The railway porter was determined not to go beyond the gate across the rails, in which there was, I think, a small wicket for pedestrians, lest he should be thought of as trying to take custom from his colleagues in the docks.

No description of the Southern Railway's fleet would be complete without a decent mention of the good ship *Winchester*. She was built in 1947 by Denny and she was very speedy, though said to do only 15 knots. Rumour has it that she was laid down as a destroyer and altered as the war ended. Her machinery was amidships, like the accommodation for twelve passengers, the maximum allowed on cargo ships. The cabins were elegant, but then they were often used by the Governors of Jersey and Guernsey. There were no jet planes to Jersey until the 1960's, or Guernsey until 1980. The Governor of each Island is appointed by the Crown, a highly paid task with a seat in the States below the Bailiff, a grand Government House, and a permanent ADC to explain things. So we travelled in style. We were invited on the bridge. There was the most disgusting smell of crude oil, both from Esso's Fawley refinery and from the Shell one on the *Hamble*. I recalled neither was there when the *St Briac* ran aground. I remarked that it could not be very nice to have to endure this pollution around, whenever he had a day off.

The Master snapped back: 'You don't suppose I live here, do you?', and I should have recognized the beak-like nose that distinguishes Jerseymen, the Originaires as they like to be known, though now outnumbered by the English, Irish, Scots and Portuguese of the 80,000-odd Jersey inhabitants. 'Steer 206' added the Master, inviting us to inspect the radar in his day cabin, which meant nothing to me, but a lot to my wife, who had been in RAF ops. signals throughout the war. 'Steer 260' replied the Quartermaster, who knew it all by heart anyway, just like the Master, momentarily forgetting his bearings, in his politeness to his guests.

I made many voyages with Captain Picot, last of the Masters to live in Jersey, and spent some jolly afternoons in various Jersey pubs when he was off duty. In the summer his ship was the *Brittany* built specially for the Jersey-St. Malo run, by Denny, for the SR in 1933. But the day of reckoning arrived in 1960 when Mr Salmon, an ex-GWR man and the BR Manager at Weymouth, succeeded in persuading BR to give up strike-ridden Southampton and run all the ships from Weymouth where there were virtually no other ships to anywhere, in 1960. The Weymouth boat trains had been moved from the GWR to the Southern line through Southampton and Bournemouth about 1956. The long meander from Bournemouth to Weymouth round by Dorchester was not electrified until after the ships had ceased using Weymouth, in 1987. In the later years when the Class '33s' were fitted with flashing lights at Weymouth Junction, for street running, it was fun on the summer night service when the boat train would suddenly appear, almost inches from the *Bistro* where the young man was entertaining his girlfriend in the romantic moonlight atmosphere, with the *Bistro's* upper rooms looking out over the quay and the yachts bobbing at the water's edge. Half the time nobody ever expected the rails to be used! Yet we all impinged on the most intimate moments, maybe a foot away from the upper windows! In 1961 the *Caesarea* and the *Sarnia* were built, by J. Samuel White in the Isle of Wight, by order of the British Government, and much to the chagrin of BR who wanted to give the order to Denny Brothers. They only lasted fifteen years because neither of the Islands were interested in having ro-ro car ferries in 1961. Older ships, *Falaise* and *Normannia*, taken off the Southampton-Le Havre and Southampton-St. Malo run, opened the ro-ro service, and rail passengers

---

BR. 21778/16

THIS TRAIN RUNS ALONG THE PUBLIC ROADWAY BETWEEN THE QUAY AND THE JUNCTION WITH THE MAIN LINE AT WEYMOUTH. PASSENGERS ARE ASKED NOT TO USE THE LAVATORIES DURING THIS PART OF THE JOURNEY.

---

no longer had refreshments west of Bournemouth. Restaurant cars used to work to Weymouth Quay from Waterloo in early Southern Region days. I had an entire tea once, between Weymouth Quay and coming off the tramway at Weymouth Junction. As for stepping off the train, three yards from the bottom of the gangway, I think of this every time I am bundled into a bus at Dover.

In 1992, I travelled in the Edinburgh-Poole sleeper to Basingstoke, not knowing it was to come off. The lady attendant refused to bring my tea before Oxford, I had to specify a time. An American lady was carried off to Reading, as the attendant refused to wake her forty-five minutes before Oxford, – she evidently did not know the line.

From Basingstoke, I set out for Salisbury in a loco-hauled Network South East train, their new Class '159s' not having arrived (at least these will have proper first class not the too-small seating, 4-a-side, provided in '158s' for runs in Scotland over 100 miles). From Salisbury I returned to Basingstoke in a two coach train hauled by a Class '33', almost the last loco-hauled non-multiple unit on the Southern – sorry, Network South East. The coaches had the unofficial names *Annie* and *Clarabel* painted on their sides, though I did not see a smiling face on the Class '33', or anyone of the girth and demeanour of the *Fat Controller* on the platform at Salisbury.

The change to the fast but uncomfortable Wessex electric set, where the only comfortable seats are in the First Class compartments, brought me back to earth. The only place in Second or Standard Class where you can stretch out, is the buffet lounge, where the bench seats encourage you not to linger. I reflected that I had not been from Salisbury to Waterloo since the day I left England for three and a half years, in 1942, about which you can read in *Gone With Regret*. Fifty years is a long time, but somehow the SR in the west has survived all the changes and upheavals of Regions, and then Sectors, while re-opened Templecombe, shut by Beeching along with the Somerset and Dorest (don't knock the Southern by saying Slow and Dirty), has won numerous best station awards. It took almost ten years to get Southampton Airport Station opened, as you can read in my book *Jersey Airlines* (still in print, published by Jersey Artists). Now it has become Southampton Parkway, it at least offers something that you used to have only from Brighton; a non-stop, sixty minute run to London.

Chapter Eleven

Glyndebourne, Glorious Glyndebourne

Nowadays Glyndebourne Opera House is being rebuilt, for yet more foreign visitors. Today it is the fashion to picnic on the grass beside the lake, where in the past few people were encouraged to do so. You were supposed to dine in the dining rooms, run in those far-off days, like *Saunton Sands Hotel* (between Barnstaple and Ilfracombe) by the owning Christie family, whose Devonshire home, near Instow also takes in guests now, in a superior, up-market way.

Glyndebourne started in 1934, and I startled everybody at West Meon by being taken to see Audrey Mildmay (Lady Christie) in *Cosi fan Tutte* (Mozart) at half-term in 1935. Nobody aged thirteen did that kind of thing. And of course Marlborough College thought any overnight absence from the place was tainting, so none was allowed and it was not possible to go again until 1938.

Unreachable directly by railway, Glyndebourne was always a place for cars. Londoners still arrive by train at Lewes, looking pretty odd in full evening dress in the middle of the afternoon at Victoria. Special Southdown coaches take them from Lewes station to the Opera House that nestles in the Sussex Downs. Pre-war, a special Pullman train ran from London to Glynde using the third 'Brighton Belle' (5-BEL) set. It stabled at Eastbourne and returned after the last service train. Motoring back to Newbury, it was always a toss-up whether you would be held at Cooksbridge level crossing, to watch the splendid thing go by, or if you got across before it. Teas were served coming down; champagne flowed throughout the journey to, as well as from, London.

I managed to escape from Marlborough in the summer of 1938, when (Sir) Peter Pears was in the Glyndebourne Opera Chorus, and Benjamin Britten came with us to watch. I little imagined that nine years would go by, and I would be working at Glyndebourne with them, but so it was in 1947. Petrol was still rationed in 1947, though as the war was over, supplies were freely available to musicians and opera singers who could obtain extra coupons to get to and from recitals, expecially if you had a 25hp 1929 Rolls-Royce which fairly drank the stuff, but used it in an elderly Morris. But supplies were not unlimited, the basic ration was severely restrictive. Private cars ran on 'white' petrol, without red dye, and petrol stations had to account in coupons for every gallon sold. The coupons all had the car's registration number on them, to help guard against their theft. But whether the car into which the petrol went, had a different number to the coupon, did not bother the petrol station, so long as the coupons tallied with the amount bought: though to do this was technically an offence, to do so by agreement with the owners of both vehicles, was totally undetectable. Far more dangerous was to put commercial petrol, dyed red, into a private car. Many people did so, as the only way to get enough petrol to manage, but 'red' petrol coupons were much more easily come by, and available on the black market. If stopped by the police and checked, a court conviction was inevitable.

1947 was also the last year of the Southern Railway Company. We all stayed at a mysterious guest house called *Bishopstone Manor*, which I believe is now pulled down and the site built all over. This meant driving every day close to nearby Bishopstone Halt on the Seaford branch, round the edge of Newhaven, keeping to the right or east side of the *River Ouse* to the neighbourhood of Southerham Junction, but bearing away to the right. Making a zig-zag crossing of the main A27 Lewes-Eastbourne road near Glynde station, we arrived elegantly, past Glynde Place, when almost everyone normally comes the other way to Glyndebourne, turning off the Lewes-Ringmer road, up over the Down. At Glynde Station, all was tranquil, with just a few coal trucks in the yard. During the war, the army had a yard there, shunted by a Dean 2301 class 0-6-0, one of many requisitioned by the War Department from the GWR, with WD and a broad arrow on the tender. Some Pullman cars were also stored at Glynde for safety, and because there was no room for them at Preston Park Works. Precisely which cars went there is not known.

In the morning we usually passed a '2-BIL' or a '2-HAL' on the Newhaven branch, but after evening rehearsals, the journey home coincided with the passage of the Up Newhaven boat train. Newhaven Harbour station was not electrified fully until 1969, and the SR only had two electric locomotives on the whole system, which were busy working the Norwood-Three Bridges-Chichester freights. So the Newhaven boat train was still steam hauled, the very last on the SR Central Section main line to Victoria.

And not any old steam: LBSCR steam, a proud 'Marsh Atlantic', usually *North Foreland* or *Beachy Head*, often tackling the heavy train alone; or sometimes taking a 4-4-0 (a 'D1' or 'E1' or SE&C origin, I think) as pilot. *Beachy Head* seemed to me very appropriately named, after the great chalk cliff between Seaford and Eastbourne, just down the coast road. Frank Bridge, the composer who taught Benjamin Britten as a schoolboy, lived at nearby Friston before the war. So boyhood memories of holidays returned, walking at dusk to hear the nightingales behind Bishopstone Manor, unsullied by noisy housing estates.

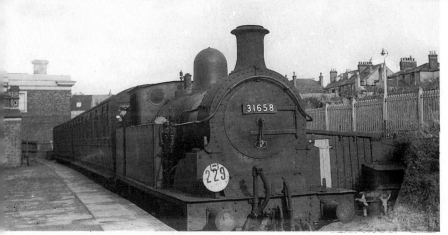

Top: '**Q1**' class 33020 rolls along beside the *Thames-Medway Canal* on the Allhallows branch train, June 1960. *D. Trevor Rowe*

Above: '**R**' class 0-4-4T No. 31658, in the bay at Gravesend Central, between trips to Allhallows-on-Sea, 2nd August 1952. *J. H. Price*

Below: '**H**' class 0-4-4T 31517 on a push-pull train at Allhallows-on-Sea in April 1960. *J. H. Price*

An Up boat train leaves Southampton Docks headed by 'Lord Nelson' 4-6-0 No. 30855 *Robert Blake*. The train is crossing Canute Road; on the right behind the advertising hoarding can be seen the roof of Southampton Terminus station, 5th April 1959. *J. H. Price*

USA' Tank, 0-6-0T No. 69, with empty boat train stock at the Royal Pier, Southampton on 21st October 1950, This locomotive which became BR No. 30069, was originally numbered 1952 by the US Army. *J. H. Meredith*

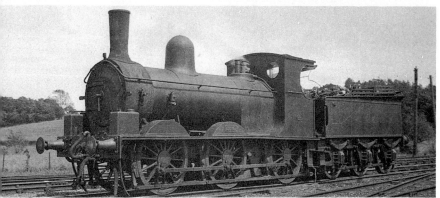

Some of Colonel Stephen's relics on the Kent and East Sussex Railway photographed in 1931.
Top: A half dismantled 'Terrier' tank loco amidst all the clutter of Rolvenden shed.
Above: No.7 *Juno*, purchased from the LSWR in 1910, outside the shed at Rolvenden.
Both W. H. Butler Collection

Below: **Hecate**, the 0-8-0T swapped by Colonel Stephens, for an ex LSWR 0-6-0 Saddle Tank, from the Southern. *J. H. Price Collection*

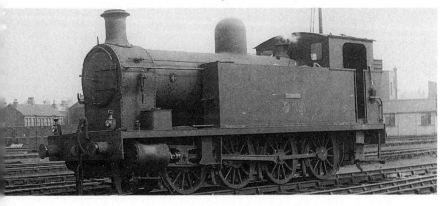

Left: **Shepperton Ferry** entering its dock at Dover in 1936. *J. H. Price*

Below: **'Le Twick', Twickenham Ferry** arriving at Dover from Dunkirk on 7th August 1972. *John Hendy*

One of Maunsell's 'N' class Moguls, A847 in its original condition without smoke deflectors. Many Swindon trained staff were to be found at Ashford and this design owed much to the Churchward 43XX Moguls of the GWR. *J. H. Price Collection*

Rush hour at East Croydon on 25th May 1953. In the foreground Ivatt's LMS designed 2-6-2T No. 41317. Beyond the signalbox, 'Schools' class 4-4-0 No. 30909 *St Pauls* on a Ramsgate to Cannon Street train and approaching the station, Brighton built BR Standard class 4 2-6-4T No. 80013. *J. H. Price*

A Western Region three-car Diesel Multiple Unit Express set (centre) at the platform on 24th December 1971. *I H Price*

Oxted line diesel units cross Riddlesdown viaduct on 19th August 1972. *J. H. Price*

Southern Railway SS *Canterbury* leaving Dover for Calais in the Summer of 1929. She is on the 12.55 departure which was for first class passengers only, who had been conveyed to Dover on the 'Golden Arrow'. The Prince of Wales Pier is on the right of the vessel.
J. H. Price Collection

Mr Smart's private saloon, originally part of the SE&CR 'Royal Train', seen at Lancing Works in 1962. *J. H. Price Collection*

The *Queen Elizabeth* at Southampton Ocean Terminal attended by 'Lord Nelson' 4-6-0 No. 30851, *Sir Francis Drake*. *J. H. Price Collection*

The Travel Bureau in the Cabin Class Reception area of the *Queen Mary*. This was run by the Southern Railway on behalf of the 'Big Four' railway companies. *Southern Railway Official Photograph – courtesy N. Norman Collection.*

Top: **'E1' class 4-4-0 passing Folkestone Warren in August 1955.** *L. Hanson*

Above: **The graceful lines of Wainright's 'E' class 4-4-0s are displayed by No. 31166 at Ashford shed on 12th September 1954.** *J. H. Price*

Below: **On 17th July 1948 'Battle of Britain' Pacific No. 21C154** *Lord Beaverbrook* **passes Cheriton with the 'Golden Arrow'.** *L. Hanson*

Rebuilt Stirling 'O1' class 0-6-0 No. 31425 shunting train ferry wagons at Hawkesbury Street Junction, Dover, 8th August 1955. Note the ship is directly behind the end wagon, beyond the long footbridge. *L. Hanson*

Southern engines regularly penetrated as far north as Oxford (*Gone With Regret:* Chapter 6).
In these two 1952 views:

Above: 'Lord Nelson' 4-6-0 No. 30864 *Sir Martin Frobisher* enters the station with a train
composed of ex LNER stock.
Below, Bulleid 'West Country' Pacific No. 34105, now preserved on the Mid Hants Railway,
at Oxford, about to leave on an inter-regional train for the Southern Region.
Both W. H. Butler Collection

The Southern Railway's new Channel Island fleet in the 1930s.

Top: **RMS *Isle of Guernsey* off St Sampson's, Guernsey.** *J. H. Price*

Above: **The RMS *Isle of Jersey*.** *George Behrend Collection*

Below: **RMS *Isle of Sark* at the Albert Quay, the SR's station in Jersey. Fitted with stabilisers, she rolled when it was calm.** *J. H. Price Collection*

Somehow the Newhaven boat train symbolised all that was going to vanish under nationalisation, though I do not recall a First Class Pullman in the train. The set comprised straight sided, 'Continental stock' and had 'Do Not Lean Out' notices in English and French ('Ne pas se Pencher au Dehors'). The Pullman was the twelve-wheel doyen of the fleet *Grosvenor*, a non-supplement buffet car with long bar counter built in 1908 and not withdrawn until after 1960. The Company was working flat out getting its cars back into service, but steam composite cars were now few, the last, *Ruth*, working the Waterloo-Southampton Docks Le Havre boat train. The train spent a long layover period at Newhaven and tying up a 1st Class Pullman all those hours was not on. But of course composites were running again in all the '6-PUL' electric sets on the Eastbourne and Littlehampton lines.

Traffic on the roads was sparse except for tractors and horses and carts, due to fuel rationing. You took risks on corners to get by, as they could not be allowed to detain important opera singers. You took your eyes off the road to look at passing trains. You knew when to expect to meet buses. I was lucky to extract a timetable from Southdown at Brighton, in those paper-rationed days, by saying I was the English Opera Group's transport manager. It bears Lord Britten's autograph, though Southdown would have been upset, had they known the main reason for wanting it!

Curiously, Benjamin Britten never once mentioned the film that the Southern Railway commissioned in 1937, for which he wrote the music. It marked the inauguration of the Portsmouth line electrification, and was called *The Way to the Sea*. Can you imagine any other railway company employing an avant garde poet like W. H. Auden, and a scarcely known, avant garde composer like Britten to make a promotional film for a new train service?

Much easier to imagine the staid, conservative Great Western scoffing disdainfully at such a notion, dismissing it briefly as typically Southern. The London and North Eastern would have been more sympathetic, but would have mentioned the hundred and one things for which they could have used the money. The righteous LMS, under the formidable Josiah Stamp (whose very Christian name makes me think of Methodism) would probably have been horrified at the extravagance, though the LMS made more publicity films than the other three railways combined, and had its own film unit.

To employ such film-makers to promote the '4-COR' sets of new rolling stock, whose frontal appearance exuded no excitement whatever, probably did not go down well with staid Southern shareholders. The '4-CORs' whose blanked off gangway end was their most prominent feature, soon earned the nickname 'Nelsons', as they only had one side front window; the other side was occupied by the route stencil.

While *Night Mail*, not of course an LMS but a Post Office film, had caused an appreciative sensation in artistic and publicity circles, and

attracted the attention of (Sir) John Elliott's 'live wire' publicity department – one might say 'live rail' were it not such a grating cliché – the
LMS got the kudos from the film due to the romanticism of steam at
night, and the Post Office did not get much. 'Waste of Government
money' was muttered here and there, though Travelling Post Offices
are a harmless enough subject; hardly box office in these violent days,
when anyway, non-stop collection and delivery of rail-born mails has
ceased altogether. The glamour provided by the locomotive contrasted
sharply with the Portsmouth electrics which looked like a corridor
coach approaching 'backwards'. Nobody ever seems to have referred
to the film since. I do know that when I suggested to the Aldeburgh
Festival that they might like to run it in 1987 in the Aldeburgh Cinema,
to celebrate the Portsmouth line electrification's golden jubilee, they
said they could not find it anywhere. In fact it is in the National Film
Archive, London, who have a viewing copy, and there is probably a
copy in the FAME film laboratory, South Norwood, which houses the
British Transport Film Library.

In those austere days, cafés had special extra food allocations to enable them to remain in business, and here one could supplement the
rations. Snatching a cup of tea in Lewes, I observed the steam East
Grinstead branch train, crossing the long demolished bridge at the bottom of Lewes High Street. Part of this route has since become a place
of pilgrimage for steam enthusiasts as the preserved 'Bluebell' line. I
overheard one customer remark that it was the slowest train in England. Much to my surprise, his companion hotly disputed this, assert-
ing the title belonged to the branch from Saxmundham to Aldeburgh in
Suffolk, a place forever associated with Britten as the location of his
opera, *Peter Grimes*, which put him on the high road to fame, if not success immediately. Aldeburgh was often in our thoughts at
Bishopstone, for we were preparing for the world première of Britten's
Albert Herring, set in an imaginary town Loxford, based partly on
Aldeburgh, where Britten had just bought a seafront house, and was
shortly to move in, from nearby Snape. I later helped Britten at the first
eleven Aldeburgh Festivals from 1948-1959.

Each day I would motor everyone to Glyndebourne, change cars
there and set off for Lewes station, to meet the London train which
hopefully would bring some more of the music. BR soon made sending
packages in guard's vans much more difficult and risky with everything taking an age to arrive or getting lost (no fax machines existed
then, and no photocopies either). We got service a smile from the
Southern Railway, so essentially a line for the people, though we took
it for granted then, not knowing what was to come. Which was just as
well, as I had no idea what music to expect and look out for. It came in
dribs and drabs as it was printed, done to suit the works and the paper
shortage. For if you can believe it, the cast were expected to rehearse
the new Opera without the music! In typical British fashion, the parts

were not ready in time! There was only Britten's handwritten full score manuscript. The finale of the Opera was written in the dressing room that I and my typewriter shared with him. Here, in the intervals between meeting trains for the hopeful arrival of more parts of the score, I endeavoured to wrestle with his burgeoning correspondence, since in those days, he had no secretary. As I was totally untrained, it was a good job presentation did not matter as it does today, and everything went off in re-used old envelopes.

Around eleven, when the morning session broke for coffee, I appeared to be the most important person in the company, as all these stars crowded round, clamouring for music which they were expected to learn in next to no time, and which was frequently not there! Somehow the cast members with the least important roles, always seemed to get theirs first! After a week of this, Glyndebourne's haughty Director, Rudolf Bing, who had been there since 1934 save for the war, and was soon to be the powerhouse and terror of the Metropolitan Opera House, New York, condescended even to say 'good morning' to me. The Glyndebourne Company was busy with Gluck's *Orfeo*, starring Kathleen Ferrier, so there was often neither stage nor music available for Britten's company, the English Opera Group, as the Glyndebourne Company was occupying the stage.

Much the hardest part of the job was taking Sir Frederick Ashton, the producer of *Herring*, to the late afternoon train at Lewes station, on days when he was performing ballet in London. (Could he not have another five minutes?). When he was returning he could not get back to Bishopstone, as the last train had gone to Eastbourne, and he had to be met at Brighton. In those austere days the last train was not the midnight one, patronized for years by Bud Flanagan and his Crazy Gang, whose pre-TV, Home Guard-style humour would scarcely raise a laugh today. The Brighton journeys were fun, and once, after a day when things had not gone well, everybody came with me, in order to greet him and to indulge in the slot machines on Palace Pier, whose ancient games had not yet gone to toy museums. It was especially amusing to think of all Ashton's ballet fans at Covent Garden, clamouring for him to take a curtain call – when he was already nearly at Victoria!

I knew Ben personally from 1936-72 and toured Scotland, Holland, Switzerland and Italy with him. In the early days, I was often mistaken for him by ignorant pressmen, which was embarassing and amusing, Britten's 1929 Rolls-Royce tourer was better known than he was!

Sussex in May is one of the best sights of Britain, and when the stage was needed for *Orfeo*'s full rehearsal, I had a day off. I went to Ore, and we shot along, over many level crossings, through Polegate with the Hailsham branch still there, round the triangle whose direct Hastings route never seemed to be much used and was lifted in the 1970s, into Eastbourne Terminus where the '6-PUL' set was left behind. On through Pevensey with all its heritage that the tourist trade had not then got round to exploiting, unlike Battle, on what is nowadays called the '1066 line', Cooden Beach, Bexhill, St Leonards West Marina, over Bo-Peep Junction with the '1066 line' (what is the origin of the name for this place?), St Leonards Warrior Square and then into Hastings. From Cooden Beach you could complete your journey to Hastings by trolleybus. Then on to Ore because there was no room at Hastings for an electric train depot. Maybe soon Ore-Ashford will be electrified now the Channel Tunnel is completed. But since they cannot move the railway forward in time to match this great creation, the word 'soon' is rather over optimistic. There is still no sign of a high speed line, though in 1992 BR has formed a subsidiary called Union Railways, to build it in partnership with private enterprise. Ashford International station is delayed, and there will be no overnight trains until 1995, though the rolling stock has been belatedly ordered at long last in 1992.

The Romney, Hythe & Dymchurch is a 15 inch gauge railway created in the 1920s. The exciting thing about the RH&D is its miniature steam. Long before American tourists came in hoards to Britain, US outline 'Pacifics' appeared on the line, one called *Winston Churchill* in view of the great man's US connections, the other named *Dr Syn*, after the most notorious of the Romney Marsh smugglers, and one of the most ruthless too, I read somewhere. It is the English style engines that are so fascinating, for not only have they several scale models of Gresley 'Pacifics', they also have the 'Mountains' that were never built in reality (nor even designed elsewhere). Such engines would have had great scope if they had been built full size, on trains like the 'Aberdonian' and the 'Night Aberdonian' from London to Aberdeen. Instead Gresley had only 2-8-2s and his successor stupidly rebuilt them. Was it not having a bogie for the many curves of the line north from Edinburgh to Aberdeen which runs spectacularly beside the sea for miles, that caused track wear and was responsible for their conversion to 'Pacifics?' or would the 4-8-2s have been too heavy for the *Forth* and *Tay* Bridges.

Sadly people forget the RH&D today, while thousands whizz off to see EuroDisney or take the 'Bluebell Line', in beautiful Sussex, handy to London and Brighton, unlike the RH&D, which is not handy to anywhere. The line on to Dungeness, fourteen miles from Hythe, is single and the the loop at the end even has sprung points. But it is remote and eerie going across the shingle where people use snow shoes to walk, shingle that is extending all the time seaward, and where there is almost nothing but an Atomic Power station. This has preserved the SR branch from Appledore on which I managed to travel from Dungeness to Lydd in 1936. It closed to passengers in 1937. At Lydd I got an East Kent double decker, one of the few Imperials ever built by Morris Commercial, marvellously smooth and comfortable, but already ousted by diesel engined buses, from having a large production run.

The journey from the pretty Hythe Terminus was behind one of the

Gresley style 4-6-2s but at New Romney we were obliged to change to one of the two trains that ran once a week for local people to go shopping. It was also the first Rolls-Royce I ever went in – or rather behind. What has happened to that splendid vehicle, which I recall, ran on bogies?

Not to have experienced the RH&D is to miss something. In those days it was much more eerie, with hardly any bungalows, south of the New Romney station. Most people seem to take preserved railways just so their children can have a steam train ride. Captain Howey built this line for fun in 1927. The late King George VI drove a train on it once (when he was still Duke of York), and it needs some more Royal patronage. Barely thirty miles from the Nazis during World War II, it had an armoured train and no doubt its guns would have been effective in an invasion. It always seemed to me a suicidal death trap, as a tank would rip up the rails through churning up the shingle, had any landed. It really is worth a special trip to see the Romney Hythe and Dymchurch Railway. The sea, the sky, the sheep, the silence, you would never know France and the Channel Tunnel were just round the corner, but then if its foggy, the silence seems to grow. Of course its broken – but by steam, beloved by all steam enthusiasts, and the line has all the amenities you'd expect, restaurant, café, gift shop – not forgetting the model layout and museum, though the other facilities duplicate themselves at Hythe, except the café, which is at Dungeness.

Hythe is one of the Cinque Ports (meaning Five Ports in Norman French) like Rye and Dover. It is old-world, and attractive to tourists from Folkestone. Though the local town East Kent buses from Folkestone run to the RH&D station, this place is curiously not visible from the road. You merely see the entrance, no inkling of those marvellous scale engines, simmering down below, the station complete with signals, turntable, signal box – and low, French style platforms. What a pity, now that Kent and Picardy are forming a common tourist region, if there are no RHDR advertisements at Noyelles on the nearest steam railway in France which is close to St Valery Sur Somme, on the coast, off the line from Boulogne to Paris. On Sundays the Baie De Somme Railway regales the passing Venice-Simplon-Orient Express with the sound of its piercing steam engine whistles.

The SR inherited Hythe's *Imperial Hotel* from the SE&C but its horse-tram to Sandgate station had ended in 1921. I never pass Folkestone, without thinking of that holiday and the Rolls-Royce RH&D engine, nor for that matter the crawl up the one-in-thirty of the Folkestone Harbour branch, sipping afternoon tea and enjoying the Devonshire cream and scones in today's VSOE Pullmans, without thinking of the five 'R1' Class 0-6-0 Tanks that used to haul up the 'Golden Arrow', on what is now BR's steepest passenger line. That is another story which belongs to the next Chapter.

Chapter Twelve

Folkestone
and the Medloc Trains

To appreciate Folkestone Harbour properly, try landing there after three and a half years away from Britain, with no home visits, stuck in the British Army overseas. Or, by way of complete contrast, arrive in style, as I did recently aboard the *SeaCat* among the Venice-Simplon-Orient Express passengers. You would be surprised how inexpensive it is to go northbound from Paris to London in this fabulous train, compared to the southbound price all the way to Venice or to Vienna and Budapest, an even greater distance (Service to these capitals suspended in 1993). World War II was a happening over which the participants in it had no control. For most people, the cities' blitz is the only part of it they remember. but many people then, like me, were not living in a city. In my case for my first year overseas I was living in a desert.

Unlike many people pre-war, who refused to believe concentration camps existed, I knew all about Nazi lists of Brits wanted for concentration camps after England was conquered (including me), compiled pre-war. You did not have to be a Jew, a German name with Jewish overtones was enough. In 1935 with my sister and a friend of ours, I visited Germany, where a Jewish doctor, friend of this friend, explained how the Frankfurt City Police, who liked his clinic and his work, rescued him through his back door, while Hitler's SA were breaking in, at the front. A year later, our friend introduced Peter Pears to Benjamin Britten, and also me to both of them!

The Medloc trains have never been fully described, perhaps because their arrangements were supposedly a military secret, even though the Army gave away maps of the journey of Medloc 'C', which served Italy. Perhaps because they served different theatres of war, I was one of the few who used more than one service. Theatres of war seem to interest politicians, historians, Defence Ministries and Foreign Offices more than ordinary folk. In UK there was no Defence Ministry until after the war, but a separate Admiralty for the Royal Navy, the War Office for the Army and Air Ministry for the RAF. Hence WD on the army engine, mentioned in Chapter Eleven. MEDLOC stood for MEDiterranean Lines Of Communication.

Field Marshal Alexander (later Lord Alexander), wanted everybody in Greece who had been abroad more than three years, to visit home by Christmas 1945. In addition, many older people and those over four years abroad, were going home for good. There were no airliners, only empty bombers. There were no buses to spare. There were few military lorries not needed for supplying occupying troops in various places.

The Eighth Army, based in Austria did arrange lorry transport at first, officially called Medloc 'B'. Eventually the main Medloc train used a similar route, starting from Villach and continuing for several years as a 'leave and duty' train for the British forces in Austria, which ceased to be occupied in 1955.

The bombers did the best they could. But they were based in Italy, and could not fly in and out of Greece, I think for political reasons, or because they might have been shot at, in the belief they had come to drop bombs. In any case, just two trips in cattle trucks (one quite illicit) constituted my entire rail travel between October 1942 and November 1945. So I was going home the proper way, by troop train.

The railways in Salonika were not working. The piles of broken rolling stock included several Wagons-Lits sleepers and diners, which upset me more than somewhat. These are recounted in *Classical Landscape with Figures* by the late *Evening Standard* cartoonist, Sir Osbert Lancaster, a reminder that Greece was having a civil war truce, while the 'Iron Curtain' was just up the line at Idomeni, on the Yugoslav, now Macedonian, frontier. Unlike everybody else, I had been that way before – by Simplon-Orient Express!

With the war over in Burma, all available troopships were needed for the soldiers there, so soldiers in Greece were taken the short trip from Athens to Taranto in the Shaw Savill liner SS *Mataroa*, the same ship that three and a half years before had taken me from Gourock near Glasgow to Durban! Soldiers in Salonika first sailed to Athens in a local military troopship whose Norwegian crew had spent the war with the Allies and were itching to go home, and whose British Military commander on board was an alcoholic.

At Taranto, after a suitable wait, the Medloc Feeder service with wooden seats for all, took us in a night, a day, and half the next night to Milan, longer than Medloc 'C' took from Milan to Calais. All this took a fortnight or so, and an Army friend, stationed at Trieste, who wrote to say he was going on leave a fortnight after me, turned up in the camp at Monza. While waiting to leave, having won the war, we decided to explore, by marching down the track from Milano Centrale station towards the flyovers at Greco. The Partisans however had other ideas, as they had captured all the lines intact from the Germans who had wished to blow them up. British officers or anybody else, not involved with the Italian State Railways, might not trespass. A few shots sent us scurrying into the suburbs.

After six years of war, it was distasteful or re-assuring, depending on your point of view, to observe that the British class system had emerged undamaged from the hostilities. There was the most fearful fuss to distinguish between officers and what the Army calls other ranks. Nobody explained why. Travelling on my own, I was asked to share with a sergeant. At the time I ran a unit of one lieutenant (me), two sergeants, six soldiers and about 150 civilians who came to work for us. Not being as snobbish as Movement Control, I saw no objection. We had a compartment to ourselves. When an officer came in, the sergeant, whom I had never seen before nor since, politely said that I was his bosom friend, just visiting. When ferocious sergeant-majors of HQ Central Mediterranean Forces, to which the sergeant belonged, tried to enter, I said 'sorry, this is an officer's compartment'. It worked very well indeed.

Best of all we went by day through Switzerland, where the Brig Stationmaster was the first person I recognized from pre-war peacetime. In the evening we were fed at Villers les Pots (Dole and Dijon near Auxonne) at a camp run for Central Mediterranean Forces by French civilians and reached by reversing onto a disused railway, and later departing by reversing onto a further loop of a disused flyover junction, most intriguing, in the dark! Next morning, I saw the officer commanding the train, jumping across the steps from our carriage to the officers coach, with hot water for the Brigadier, to shave with. I noticed it was French, unlike all the Italian carriages in the rest of the train, and the gangways would not fit. All the officers except me, had had to get up at four in the morning and change into it, as their coach had broken down!

Soon, we diverted off the main line to Calais, and went to Epluches, near Pontoise where we had breakfast at a camp, run by the British Army of the Rhine. This was craftily situated to feed everybody bound for either Dieppe, or Calais, from everywhere; Milan (Medloc 'C'), Toulon (Medloc 'A' for Middle and Far East Forces), and Rhine Army leave and duty trains, which were not part of Medloc.

We had stopped to change engines at every place of note, and when I asked why, it was explained that otherwise a good engine would disappear, and an old crock would be returned in exchange. Adjacent depots could not do this, as if they did, they would simply have their old crock returned on the next service, or if a good one, not returned until the depot got its own good engine back.

Calais was a wreck. We were marched to army huts, passing the Wagons-Lits' local office, which was a teak sleeper with all the details in Polish. I tried and failed to memorise the impossible Polish for 'Wagons-Lits' as we marched by, tantalisingly – twice. It was impossible to stop, or write it down. We were ferociously guarded like criminals by British Army of the Rhine's Military Policemen, who had no time at all for soldiers who had been away from home for years before their precious D-Day invasion. Officers were even worse, they were thought liable to abscond.

Notices in the huts threatened to deprive offenders from ever leaving BAOR for beloved 'Blighty' as every serviceman calls England when overseas, or alternatively ever getting back to the relative comfort of the part of the army to which they belonged. The reason for this draconian behaviour was that the camp authorities and staff had no idea how long their inmates would be staying, and the inmates refused to believe they genuinely did not know! Hot water for washing or shaving was a dream in the Calais camp, which I luckily missed on all subsequent Medloc journeys.

We sailed from Calais to Folkestone, a route never used pre-war, and abandoned when every cross-channel steamer had become a roll-on, roll-off car ferry. We crossed in the *Biarritz*, (built in 1914, the oldest member of SR fleet), once again, class distinction made me angry. Why, I enquired, none too obsequiously, were only officers allowed on deck? Military Orders were one thing, SR high-handedness quite another. The Boatswain was quite explicit: 'With this load on, Sir, if everyone were allowed on deck, as soon as she started rolling, she'd roll over!'

On my return from leave, I saw an Army Notice, that I have never forgotten, at the *Burlington Hotel*, Folkestone, where the Army received us, saying that if you had not been abroad before, you would not have to go because your overseas service would be cut short by demobilisation, but if you had been years away from home, you must go abroad again. It permanently altered my outlook on Britain. No reason was given for this monstrously unfair treatment, allowing people who had never been away or back every six months as in BAOR, to secure the right contacts for jobs.

Nearly thirty years went by before I found out about the class distinction on the trains. To get everybody home by Christmas, meant moving 100,000 people in a very few weeks. The Swiss were very co-operative, the war being over, and their neutrality intact. They supplied two whole Swiss Medloc Trains (there were twenty trains alone on Medloc 'C'), and they only charged 1939 fares, First Class for officers, Third Class for the rest. The only stipulation was that payment had to be in . . . gold francs, not Swiss francs! Consequently H.M. Treasury was displeased, and in 1946, as a result, the Medloc route from Italy was closed down. People from Austria went by Germany from Villach, Greece was reclassified as part of the Middle East again, as in 1941, so people from Greece went by sea from Athens to Toulon.

The Royal Navy, responsible for the safe passage at sea of the Army and the Royal Air Force personnel, would suddenly announce that the weather was too rough for sailing. Not because nasty little ships like the *Biarritz*, built – how did you guess? – by Wm. Denny of Dumbarton (for the South Eastern & Chatham Railway) – were not perfectly able to sail overloaded, whatever the weather, but because there were stray mines floating about, that had broken loose from uncleared minefields, in rough weather.

Operating the service was thus something of a miracle, performed at Allied Force Headquarters, Central Mediterranean Forces by Major Mike Marshall of the Royal Engineers. He explained to me (by lending me a document) how he arranged for troops to be temporarily billeted in camps along the way, so as not to have hundreds of troops arriving at the same time in trains at Calais, where the camps were already full. Luckily I did not know all this at the time, as I had my own problem, to work my 1946 homecoming so that the arriving leave they gave, coincided with the brief fortnight of Britten's Opera, *The Rape of Lucretia*, at Glyndebourne. All I knew was that the secret of comfortable Medloc travel was to stop as long as possible at every camp along the way, where you could freely go out in the local towns – in those days perfectly safe – and none of this counted against your leave, which started at Folkestone (or Dover), on the day you arrived.

I managed, with some luck, to get my trip to Glyndebourne, little thinking that within a year I would be working with the Opera there.

MAP OF MEDLOC 'C' ROUTE
Milan – Calais
used by Central
Mediterranean Forces Italy

My travelling companion was a Colonel, a regular army doctor, who made my life hell for the last few weeks in Greece, without telling me of his fear that something would go wrong and we would both be delayed in leaving our respective units. He used me as a private ADC until we got off the ship at Toulon, where he whizzed off on the first available train, whereas I waited for the last one. This Medloc 'A' service ran daily until a troopship was unloaded, and then stopped altogether, so there were only 169 passengers on a train able to take 600. This time I shared with a Royal Navy officer, much impressed with my sheets and blankets; the sheets came from Egypt, in 1943. Medloc 'A' had originally had meal stops at Bram near Carcassone and Neuvy Pailloux near Vierzon, but these had been replaced by just one at Brive, when I travelled.

Not exactly 'Le Train Bleu' or the 'Flanders-Riviera' as the Calais-Nice sleeper runs today, and the journey took two nights and a day, as the line from Paris to Lyons was about to be electrified and SNCF were

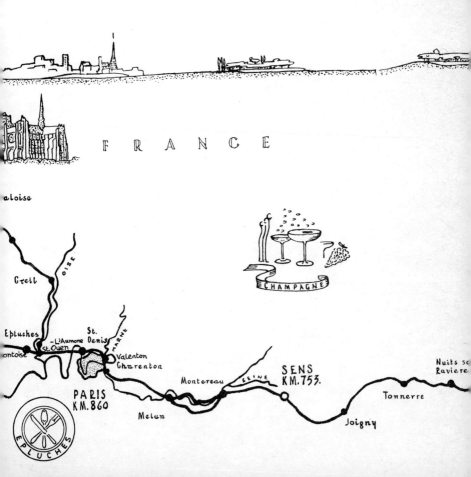

short of steam locomotives. So we went for a circular tour of France via Marseilles (Blancard), Tarascon, Sète, Narbonne, Toulouse, Brive, Limoges, Valenton, Chantilly, Creil, Amiens. Epluches had closed down and we stopped only once, at Brive La Gaillard where we were fed in a French army barracks, conveniently rail-connected. The train was electrically hauled from Sète to near Valenton. The SNCF went on strike at midday the second day, but exempted Medloc trains. So we batted along at around 60 mph (steam hauled of course – I think by a '141R' class 2-8-2) with clear signals from Amiens. This time we went straight on to Dover. Here the Army motored us to the Castle, and after 'processing' we were sent off by ordinary train from Dover Priory.

This was a big contrast to the 1945 Folkestone arrival which was as one had dreamed for almost four years. Straight off the boat, a nominal Customs inspection, and onto the boat train, where three 'R1' class 0-6-0 tanks were attached to the front, and two more behind. Pre-war they managed with three. The driver of the front one was well over

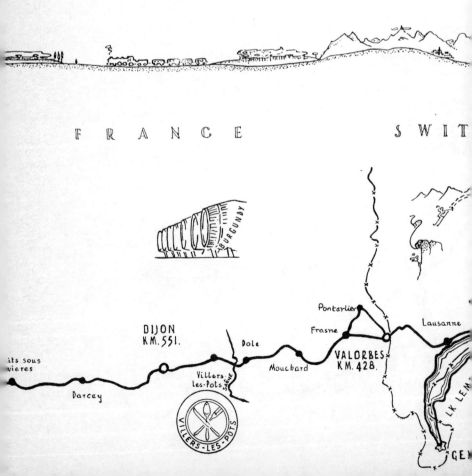

seventy, assisted by a fireman who was a small boy when the war started. Stupidly, I suggested they were very busy, with several more boat trains evident on the sidings on the shore, now the car park, and extra ships like the *Biarritz* for troops, as well as the civilian ones. The man snorted: 'He's seen nothing yet' indicating to his fireman, 'now in the last war . . . ' Only the teacups, rattling with the fore and aft motion of climbing up the Tramroad as it is called, and the tea so dexterously poured despite the lurches, were missing, like the Pullman cars.

Waiting for us at the top was 850, 'Lord Nelson' herself. How disappointed I would have been had it been one of Mr O. V. S. Bulleid's Spam Cans, as non-Southern people disdainfully called his Merchant Navy 'Pacifics'. The driver leaned leisurely out of the cab, as we struggled by, up the final grade of one in thirty to the dead end junction sidings. The two rear 'R1s' retreated down the Tramroad again, to haul the next empty boat train from the shore sidings. No. 850 set back onto the train, as soon as they were clear. I looked at my watch. We were, I

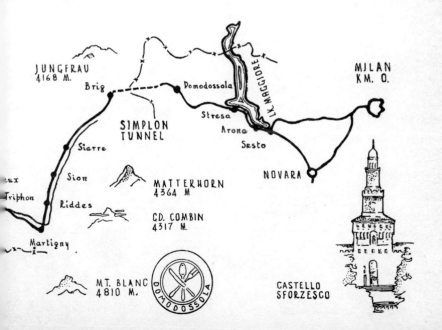

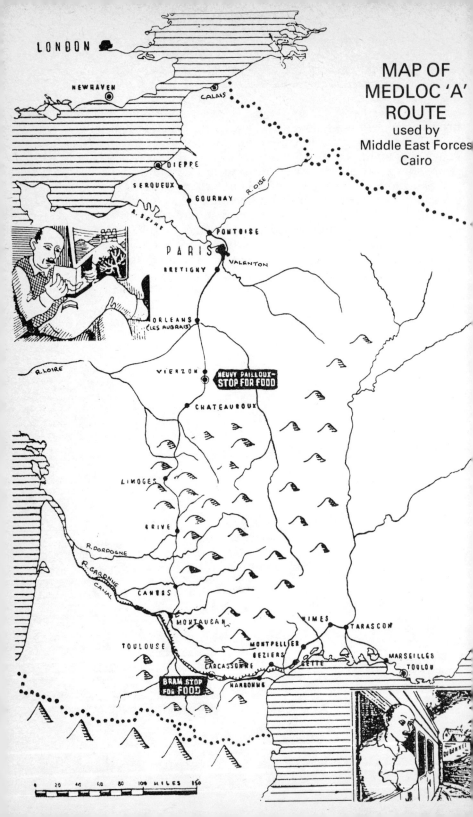

was amazed to see, within a few minutes of the Up pre-war 'Golden Arrow's' path, with the right engine too, for of course the 'Arrow' was not yet back in service. It re-started in 1946, – and was spryly taken by my RN officer companion from Toulon, who saw it standing in Dover Marine. He did not have to report to anybody at Dover.

The other officers in my carriage, who came on leave every six months or so, found travelling banal, one train was the same as another. But after Ashford, yes, there was 'Terrier' No.3 at Headcorn on the afternoon Kent & East Sussex train. The idea of nationalising it, and of Mrs Barbara Castle shutting it down, never crossed my mind. Now a factory stops it being put back, but at least the K&ESR will be able to extend to Robertsbridge on the Hastings line, as soon as they get the funds to build the line on from Northiam.

It is reckoned that something like three million people used the Medloc trains to get home, between 1945 and 1955, and the vast majority of these completed their journeys in the familiar comfort of a Southern carriage. The SR's achievement in transporting the escapees from Dunkirk is well known. It is time that the SR's contribution at the end of the war to the Medloc epic, is fully acknowledged. As this book was about to go to press, plans were announced for a Medloc 50th Anniversary Steam Train. It is proposed to run a commemorative train, in May 1995 over the original route of Medloc 'A', from Toulon to Dieppe via Marseilles, Arles, Nimes, Montpellier, Narbonne, Carcassonne, Toulouse, Cahors, Brive, Chateauroux, Vierzon, Orleans (Les Aubrais), Etampes, Paris (Valenton), Pontoise, Gisors, Gournay and Dieppe. The trip will take four days and the motive power engine will be an oil fired 2-8-2, No.141R 1126, one of over 1000 built in US and Canada around 1944 for SNCF to relieve their engine shortage.

One wonders for the well-being of the Folkestone Harbour swing bridge, after Network South East played trains with it for steam enthusiasts in 1991, using a 'Battle of Britain' 4-6-2 and a BR 2-6-4T and on only one of the two lines on the bridge; West Meon's lopsided stresses all over again! For though the line was to shut completely, when Sealink ended its ship service from Boulogne at the end of the year, it is now in full use again for the *SeaCat* Catamarans on the route. The *SeaCats* began running in April 1992 and are used to take passengers on the Venice-Simplon-Orient Express across the Channel.

It happened that I was on the very first Folkestone-London trip of the Venice-Simplon-Orient Express in 1992, which is how I know there was a delay on the outward service, caused by BR allowing the Folkestone Junction points to rust up solid, between January and April. Gangers had to be sent for, so Folkestone East signal box could work them! So don't knock the Southern, at least we were not faced with that embarrassing problem in 1945.

Chapter Thirteen

Isle of Wight Day Trip

The Isle of Wight Railways had always been held up as quaint, since they were taken over by the Southern, when previously they had been independent. Suddenly here was Beeching, advocating their extinction, and it seemed bizarre, never to have visited the Island.

One Sunday morning in the late 1950s I set off from 'Waterloo to Portsmouth & Isle of Wight' as it would have said on the roofboard in the days when there were some, although the train did not go there. I always thought this misleading, like the 'Guernsey and Jersey' labels on the Channel Island boat trains. Though nearly ten years had gone by since nationalization, the trains were still painted green, and the trip to Portsmouth was all that the slick Southern Electric should be. We called at Guildford, climbed to Haslemere, meandered to stops at Liphook and Liss, and arrived at Petersfield.

Then on, down the hill which had been a challenge to Mr Drummond's 4-4-0s. East Hampshire is a place apart, very pleasant, and 'very nearly Sussex'. Round the corner into Havant station, with a 'Terrier' on the Hayling Island train. Next, on through Fratton to the complicated Portsmouth and Southsea station whose lower platforms seemed little used, and thus to Portsmouth Harbour.

Portsmouth Harbour station at the end of the peninsula, exists mainly for the Isle of Wight, and also the Gosport Ferry. Faced with competition from the Red Funnel steamers from Southampton, the SR was always keen on snappy service; off the train, down the ramp, onto the steamers which seemed to be 'mini-Cross-Channel' ones, with all the same appointments except cabins, and all the same smells, varnish, paint, hot oil, calculated with some vibration to produce the 'undesired effect'.

I was surprised how relatively long it took, but then we were tied up at Ryde Pier, and here was the second surprise, that unheard noise I had half forgotten, the panting of Westinghouse air pumps. The engines, of course they were 0-4-4 tanks, looked smaller than the ones on the mainland, and they obviously had not always had air brakes, now fitted specially, surely, for service in the Island. The slightly sloping smokebox door seemed somehow familiar. They were of course

Adams '02' class. But how many there were! One arriving, two ready to leave, all out to sea, supported by wooden posts, the wooden jetty was iron clad to strengthen it. A terrific smell of sea, wisps of steam blowing about, no wonder people like sailing, with all this wind around.

I decided to go to Ventnor, wanting to see the south of the Island. Alongside the track was the tramway, owned and operated by the Southern, and it seemed a very long way to dry land at Ryde Esplanade, and on in a tunnel to Ryde St Johns Road. I remember a large piece of double-single track to save on junction signal boxes. Sandown struck me as a nice place for a holiday, at least you can still get there on the Southern in their hand-me-down London Underground trains, converted to third rail. Finally a deep tunnel under Ventnor, landing us in a steep sided cutting with little room to run round, because a building was in front. We were there so short a time it made no lasting impression. At any rate, the end points for running round were fixed like a turntable segment. The service was too dense for any push-pull auto-trains, and only two '02s' were so fitted, I believe, for use on the line to Freshwater. There seemed to be a great number of competing Southern Vectis buses, great Bristol double deckers with full height bodies. This Company was formed by the Southern when they bought Dodson Brothers of Newport. Though the SR immediately transferred fifty percent of the equity to the Thomas Tilling group, the Company's registered office remained at Waterloo Station until 1935, the only bus company in Britain to have its registered office in a railway headquarters.

When the SR steamers became Sealink, everything stayed very Southern until Sealink in turn was sold, for something of a song to Sea Containers. That company retained the IOW services (using the name Wightlink for them) when it sold the rest of Sealink to the Swedish Stena Line. But this was all in the future as I looked at the familiar buff-funnels of SR ships, as we approached Ryde Pier, after my return trip behind the '02'. The Pier had a Southern atmosphere of slam doors, and panting engines, almost a mini-commuter service.

My main worry was to get back off the Island, in time to re-book at Portsmouth Harbour and catch the train, which was a return excursion from Swindon, Didcot, and intermediate stations to Newbury and Winchester. I was not sure if I had caught an early enough ferry, especially as none was waiting when I reached Ryde Pierhead.

Still, it was fascinating to see all this busy Sunday activity. When a train arrived another 0-4-4T coupled on to the front of its coaches and the set was thus quickly ready to depart again. The engine that had brought the train in, followed out behind to take water, and loiter about for the next lot of trains, which arrived more or less simultaneously to suit the ferries. My Ventnor one happened to be first train to arrive. The coaches were non-corridor, bogie stock. The scale of the bustling SR Island service made me realise that for forty years I had never understood how large the SR really was. It always seemed tiny in the south and south east, while the withered arm was so infernally withered and roundabout, that you either went by GWR or you motored, unless you had all day to travel. But there was no pause at Portsmouth Harbour. SR Inspectors blew whistles, as at Dover Marine or Victoria, and people hurried into the Southern Electric for Waterloo in those '4-COR' units that somehow lacked the glamour they ought to have had, because, try as the SR might to unite the service, the IOW was somehow apart; different and self-sufficient in outlook from commuter trains to the 'Smoke', as Hampshire people still called the 'Metropolis', which you and I call simply 'London', today.

Anyway, here goes: 'Single to Highclere', I said nonchalently to the booking clerk at Portsmouth Harbour, now that Highclere was in the Southern Region, he ought to have a fare. He had. I paid so many shillings and thought I had made it, when the man suddenly remembered that the Didcot, Newbury and Southampton still had no Sunday trains. 'How are you going to get there?' he shouted at me. I pointed at the nice GWR 43xx Mogul sizzling on its chocolate and cream train which was quite long enough to be mistaken for a Reading train via Basingstoke. I hoped nobody would prevent me boarding this return excursion, for never before had I ever taken these rare trips to the Island which the GW had sometimes provided. At a time when BR was shutting buffet cars in train sets on Sundays, behold this one, doing big business in beer. They also had some very splendid Meursault which came from the GWR cellars at Swindon, of which I had little notion: I thought everything was done at Paddington, in the bottling line.

Anyway I caught it, and soon we were away, calling only at Fareham and Eastleigh before swinging off the London to Bournemouth main line, at Shawford Junction onto the erstwhile Didcot, Newbury and Southampton line which was now part of the Southern Region. We stopped at Winchester Chesil, as BR had carefully renamed it, and paused to set down at all the stations. Somehow that Meursault was extra special. In thirty-four years, this was the only time I'd travelled in a dining car to my home station at Highclere, I never thought it possible.

The foregoing gives, I think, an idea of how the Island looks to visiting mainlanders. All too often, such people wish to attach the Isle of Wight as a sort of appendage to something else; they do not understand at all, the feelings of the people who live there, never having lived on an island, as I have.

Dr, later Lord Beeching's plan was to keep the Ryde Pierhead-Ryde Esplanade (with Bus Interchange) -Ryde St John's Road portion of railway, and sweep all the rest away. The Ryde service was to be run with former London electric tube trains, but fitted with diesel engines. Thanks largely to the initiatives of the London Transport engineers at Acton Works, it was then found that they could electrify the line by converting the tube trains to work on the third rail. The London Underground uses four rail track, with a return rail separate from the running lines. The Isle of Wight has always had mainland cast-offs, since before their railways were grouped with the Southern, so more second hand stock caused no geat surprise.

The Tubes arrived in the Isle of Wight in 1967. BR had its railway and Beeching had to be propitiated by shutting down the rest. Ideas that enthusiasts might perpetrate steam when BR had just shown it was willing to pay out money to modernise, even with elderly electrics, were unacceptable. They abhorred the enthusiasts, especially as most of them were not Islanders but Londoners, and they cut off the junction at Smallbrook without any warning. At a stroke they separated the Adams '02' No. W24 *Calbourne* which was in store at Ryde, from the carriages, stored at Newport. The line to Newport shut down in February 1966, and it took until 1969 to get the money and a suitable low loader to shift the engine. It was passed as usable in 1970.

Mr Ashby, whom we met in Chapter Seven, had a scheme for reopening the railway from Ryde to Newport, but when vandals wrecked his railcar that was the end of that. It did, however stop BR lifting the track. Readers of *Gone With Regret* will recall that they did this in Devon to the pretty Kingsbridge Branch with its great tourist potential, only seven days after the last through Kingsbridge-Paddington train of the summer season.

Sadler-Vectrail, as Mr Ashby's IOW organization was called, announced in September 1970 that they would not proceed, so BR was very eager to tear up the track, demolish the stations and generally make sure Beeching's plans were fulfilled. (Though of course BR never says such things; it wishes to avoid paying rates on its property, and general losses on surplus assets).

Having succeeded in preventing BR tearing down Haven Street Station, the starting point selected by the Wight Locomotive Society for running their trains for fun over a short distance towards Newport, BR turned the Society out of Newport Station where all their rolling stock was situated. They got just five days notice. But by this time, three quarters of the Society were Islanders, and there was no shortage of volunteers. No. W24 *Calbourne* was able to run, and haul the stock away. But Haven Street had no sidings to speak of, everything had to be stored in the open, and there was more trouble at the other end of the line, because the weather caused a landslip in a cutting. So a new station had to be constructed, at Wootton.

All these efforts were backed up by the Island authorities. The Isle of Wight's trade is tourism. For years it had been at a great disadvantage to the Channel Islands, since it had no airport and it took an hour or more to cross to the Isle of Wight, the same time as it took to fly to the Channel Islands. The enterprising Southern Railway had filled this gap too, in the 1930s, starting its own air service from Southampton to

Ryde. Soon afterwards this was amalgamated with the GWR air service across the Bristol Channel, to form Railway Air Services Limited. The SR played a leading role in this; it acquired Jersey Airways to form Channel Islands Air Services. But the Isle of Wight air service did not continue during, nor after the war.

Hovercraft services to the Island started in 1965. They do the trip from Ryde Quay Road to Southsea Clarence Pier in just ten minutes. New Hovercraft were built in the Isle of Wight in 1989/90. The landing apron at Ryde was enlarged in 1991 and a new terminal building at Southsea opened, twice the size of the earlier one. As four craft are available (two built in the 1980s), Hovertravel are well placed to meet the competition from the ferry companies, who now run Catamarans for passengers taking fifteen to twenty minutes – and in the case of Wightlink, connect properly at Portsmouth Harbour or Ryde Pier with BR Network South East. The Hovercraft Terminal, Ryde BR Esplanade Station at the landward end of the Pier, and the Southern Vectis Bus Station all sensibly adjoin. The main attraction of IOW tourism is a throwback to the 1950s-60s, with an abundance of open top double deck buses, taking you along pretty cliffs belonging to a large extent to the National Trust and visiting a plethora of wildlife or rural life attractions, plus the railway.

The Isle of Wight Steam Railway really got going in the 1970s, getting a Light Railway Order in 1978. The County Council had already bought the track. In the 1960s old engines were considered artistic static monuments in pubs and holiday camps that also could amuse the kids. But as they began rusting away, the owners were happy to get rid of them. Brickwoods Brewery, taken over by Whitbread, ceased to need a 'Terrier' at Havant at the *Hayling Billy* pub. Whitbreads gave it to the railway. This engine had been running pre-war on the Island, as had another 'Terrier', which had also been on the Hayling Island branch, and was rescued from Butlin's Pwllheli Holiday Camp.

One preserved railway is much like another. The British Tourist Authority and the English Tourist Board aim to have one within sixty miles of every large English urban community. The Great Little Trains of Wales consortium of narrow gauge lines has put much of Wales on the map – people drive there with ease. Though there are three car ferries to the Isle of Wight, it is a performance; you must book; or queue; or both, and the ferries take thirty-five minutes to an hour They run Portsmouth-Fishbourne, Lymington-Yarmouth (Wightlink) and Southampton-East Cowes (Red Funnel). If you want to see the SR at work like it was, there is the 'Bluebell', handily placed – one would say 'twixt' London and Brighton, were it not such a formidable adman's word today.

The idea of journeying to the Island, taking a bus to Haven Street just for a mile and a half of train, certainly limited things. Especially as most probably the engine might not be SR at all, but an industrial loco. All steam railways arm themselves with these reliable machines. Young people want a steam train – any steam will do. The railway finally got their Wootton Station finished in 1986 and had the sense to ask the then Managing Director of Network South East, Chris Green, to open it.

Mr Green gave the railway the clout and push it needed with large concerns like BR and Wightlink, and bodies like the Rural Development Commission. Luckily no obstructions had been built on the track bed and so volunteers began relaying in 1989, after Mr Green had set up the Wight Steam Link Consortium to link the railway with the BR line at Smallbrook Junction. But Smallbrook Junction had no station, so BR built one for £185,000 and you cannot reach it by road – or even by foot. It was opened on 20th July 1991 and now at a very moderate cost there is an all day rover ticket for as many journeys as you like on both. On the BR line the Network Railcard is valid, if you have one, but not on the Steam Railway. In the first year since the line reached Smallbrook Junction, they reckon nearly a quarter of the Isle of Wight Steam Railways visitors came by BR train instead of car or bus. Wightlink, Red Funnel and Southern Vectis plus the Council all helped with the cost of the three and a half miles of new track, totalling £600,000.

The only other place where you can go in a BR tube train, as opposed to a London Underground one, is the Waterloo and City Railway. The SR built new cars for this just at the outbreak of World War II and they were delivered from Eastleigh in 1941. For this purpose, the LSWR who bought the railway in 1907, and had been associated with it from its commencement in 1898, installed a hoist at Waterloo near the Windsor lines. Routine maintenance is done at the level of the running line, under the Thames to the Bank Station. It was only the second tube in London, following the City & South London Railway. But the hoist has got in the way of the new Waterloo International station for Channel Tunnel trains, so it has been removed. New rolling stock is delivered by road and lowered into the tube by mobile road crane. As new rolling stock supplied in 1991-2 for this line is technically similar to new tubes being built for the London Underground, it seems likely it will be repaired at their Acton Works when major overhauls are needed, rather than Eastleigh. So possibly London Transport, parent of London Underground Limited, will take it over, though nothing has been said about it.

Meanwhile in the Isle of Wight, 1938 Tube stock from the Bakerloo line arrived in the island in 1990, and has been formed into nine trains of two cars. They operate every twenty minutes, sometimes more frequently and at winter slack times, less so. The cars were the first steel stock to be unpainted, bringing the 'silver trains' to the Island. The quality of construction of Metropolitan Cammell Carriage & Wagon Company in the 1930s was outstanding, and though they are over fifty years old, they will probably last for years. BR in the Island has its own works repair shops, and the Islanders have a long tradition of using second hand mainland rolling stock.

But if you wish to experience what trains were like before grouping, then the Isle of Wight Steam Railway is where to do it, as all the carriages belonged to either the SE&C, LBSC or the Isle of Wight Central. Now they want more coaches; they have the bodies but the underframes are second hand. They are not yet working, but soon will be. The two 'Terriers', W8 *Freshwater* and W11 *Newport* have a lengthy history. The Adams '02' 0-4-4T is the only survivor of its class.

The Isle of Wight is very much unto itself, proud of Cowes week, proud of Queen Victoria's *Osborne House*, proud of its rural, unspoilt coastline, and so the Steam Railway paints one of the 'Terriers', which the Isle of Wight Central bought off the LBSCR, in IWC, rather than SR colours. People like to think that life is better than on the mainland, though all islands have their limitations. Not least of these is that it always seems more difficult for Island residents to leave, than it is for visitors to visit the Islands.

But perhaps most of all, it is English, though moving with the times. The Southern Vectis bus timetable has a preface in French, German and Dutch for visitors. The 1992 cover shows two 1950 buses on their vintage circular Route 8 squeezing past swarms of tourists between thatched cottages, one of which is called *Tea Gardens*. Even the sheep next door are having tea – while opposite, somebody inside the picturesque thatched dormer windows is busy sprinkling water on a tourist whose camcorder is pointed directly at their sitting room.

Chapter Fourteen

The Last Train to Paris

'For the last time' boomed the announcer at Victoria Station, on 31st October 1980, 'The 'Night Ferry' through sleeping cars to Paris and Brussels will leave from Platform 2 at 21.25'.

Of course there was no diner, so it was necessary to patronise the *Grosvenor Hotel* at Victoria, which has a special entrance onto the platforms, as well as the main one in Buckingham Palace Road. In those days it still belonged to British Transport Hotels, part of the 'Etap' hotel chain, whose Paris director, Philip Jefford of Wagons-Lits, was largely responsible for my presence.

We had arrived at Victoria in a private omnibus, which seemed suitable style. In fact it was a former Thomas Tilling AEC petrol engined open staircase *Regent* of 1929-30 such as graced the streets of south east London, including Victoria, and those of Brighton and Hove, as mentioned in Chapter Four. Its number was ST922 in London Transport's 1933 classification, and it is the only time I have ever been anywhere in my own private double decker.

On the screen at Victoria Station which usually proclaimed delays and diversions, were the words 'Au Revoir, Mon Ami', and a repeat of the station announcement. Not 'Adieu'? Was this BR crocodile tears or connected with the rumour that an American businessman would buy all the cars and restore them? Sadly we know he did not, but, instead, re-created the Simplon-Orient Express between London and Venice – though he did buy just one 'Night Ferry' sleeper, which has remained unrestored ever since. In the process he virtually restored the 'Golden Arrow', which departs once more from Platform 2, just as it did until 1939, with elegant Pullman cars including three from the 1951 'Golden Arrow' formation itself.

On 7th February 1992, twelve years after destroying the 'Night Ferry', BR announced that new sleeping cars for cross-Channel through night trains had finally been ordered! They are planned to start in 1995, although the Tunnel will be ready in 1993. It is however French Railways (SNCF) that is lukewarm over sleeping cars, because, in France for a hundred years they have been operated or staffed by the Wagons-Lits Company, and SNCF has no sleeping car conductors of its own, unlike BR. The first new overnight sleepers from London will not run to Paris, but to Amsterdam; and to Frankfurt or Dortmund via Cologne. Through services are also planned from Glasgow, Cardiff and Penzance to Brussels and Paris, a service which will mean shunting, which BR tries to avoid at all costs, to save expense. However, much of the shunting is likely to be done by the SNCF, near Calais.

When the Wagons-Lits contract for the service was not renewed in 1976, SNCF at the same time took over responsibility for maintenance and repair of sleeping cars based in France, and Wagons-Lits' large works at St Denis, outside Paris, was closed. Formerly it could repair thirty-eight cars simultaneously, but it has now been pulled down and the site used for something else, non-railway associated. The second Wagons-Lits works (but not the carriage sheds that house the 'Blue Train' to the Riviera) at Villeneuve Prairie, also just outside Paris, was closed too. Most of the sleeping cars in France belonged to SNCF but some, including the 'Night Ferry' cars still belonged to Wagons-Lits and were leased. SNCF having no attendants of their own, BR attendants had to take over the staffing of the 'Night Ferry' from 1977-1980.

The 'Night Ferry' need not have stopped running, its fare at £66 was ridiculously low at a time when an hotel room cost around £50 per night in London. European Community money was available for new cars, and new sleepers were ordered by BR around 1980 for internal services (the Mark III that now run all BRs services). This would have enabled the Members of the European Parliament and others who used the Brussels service, to have continued to do so. Restoration of Car 3792, which was presented to the National Railway Museum York by Wagons-Lits, cost £12,500. It arrived a year or two before the train ended. £500,000 would have refurbished the whole fleet, in Wagons-Lits' Ostend (Belgium) works.

The 'Night Ferry' was a private enterprise train, started by the Southern, together with the Nord Railway (France) and the Wagons-Lits Company. Wagons-Lits means Sleeping Car in Belgian-French patois, for the Company was founded in Belgium in 1876 and taken over in 1991 by the French Accor Hotel Group. The French for Sleeping Car is 'Voiture-Lits'. The service started on 14th October 1936 after some trials a few days earlier and details of my first trip on it are in Chapter Nine. The Nord Railway became part of the nationalized SNCF in 1937/8. During World War II the service was suspended from 3rd September 1939 until 7th December 1947, when it was got going again by the Southern Railway a few days before it was in turn nationalized on 1st January 1948. Under nationalization all existing contracts were honoured and BR had to put up with a private enterprise service whose First and Second Class through passengers were partially subsided by the Third Class, who sat up all night and changed trains at the ports. There was thus a pre-war standard of comfort, privacy and service on BR's tracks in the case of the 'Night Ferry', for those who could afford it, so different to the concept of the social railway, beloved of many. The contract lasted until 1961 and as mentioned in Chapter Four was extended until 1976.

By 1980 the 'Night Ferry' was not just the only BR international train that crossed the Channel. It was over thirty years old. With the abolition of Second Class in 1956, when Third Class became, first Second, and then on BR, Standard, the 'Night Ferry' became First Class only, and in 1980 was the sole First Class accommodation available on board any Sealink ship on the Channel service. It had supplementary fares, too, which are not liked by British travellers and which BR tried to abolish.

But though we arrived as directed, half an hour before departure time at Victoria Station, BR showed its real appreciation of First Class fare-paying passengers by herding them behind a barrier and refusing to let them board, though the time was after 21.00. So the nostalgic atmosphere was rather spoilt by the vociferous passengers, particularly a British one who was ashamed at the treatment of the foreign enthusiasts, one of whom had come specially from Zurich to experience the train!

BR blamed the Customs, the Customs blamed the Railway Police, who patiently, though they would dearly have preferred to arrest this vociferous Brit for disturbing the peace, explained that the single Immigration Officer provided, had not yet shown up, so we all had to wait, fuming.

When, at last, we were permitted to board, behind the '73' class electro-diesel which had brought the train in from Grosvenor Road carriage shed, there was the nostalgic sight of seven Wagons-Lits cars, all in the Company's colours and none repainted in SNCF livery. The two vans, which carried the mail, belonged to SNCF and were in their colours. It recalled the thrill of seeing the proud title 'Compagnie Internationale des Wagons-Lits Et Des Grands Express Européens' on the very same rolling stock, forty-three years earlier, though the last five words had been omitted, ever since 1967.

Having withdrawn all the '71' class (later '74' class) electric locomotives that used regularly to haul the train, seven full sleepers were regarded as too heavy for a '73' electro-diesel, so though the third rail had been extended to Dover almost twenty years before, BR wastefully used a diesel, No.33 043 thus ensuring that the maximum operating costs were incurred to the end. To make sure the train ran at a loss, passengers not using the sleepers, were conveyed separately, and the guard was given a whole bogie composite coach to himself, which had to be detached at Dover.

As a nice gesture, in place of the oblong headboard used on the electrically-hauled train, somehow the famous round one that had so long adorned the smokeboxes of innumerable L1 4-4-0s which piloted the 'West Country' or 'Battle of Britain Pacifics' until 1959, was secured to the front. I wondered if the engine would run round the triangle out-side Southern House as the old *Lord Warden Hotel* was now called, to avoid moving the board for the inward service. This was actually worked by what is usually regarded as the 'Royal Train' engine for this part of England's 'Royal Trains', a '73' class electro-diesel No.73 142 *Broadlands*. It is named after the palatial home near Romsey of the late Lord Louis Mountbatten, where both Her Majesty the Queen, and the Prince of Wales, spent part of their respective honeymoons.

The driver of 33 043 kindly told us that this run would be by the time honoured way through West Dulwich, Herne Hill, Bickley Junction, Orpington, Tonbridge and Folkestone. But as usual, the press were far more interested in the passengers, such as the two young gas fitters on their first and last trip, next to my compartment, or the last-minute travellers who had heard of the train's demise on the radio, and had gone off there and then.

Their discovery that ordinary folk like travelling First Class, diverted the press from asking about Her Majesty the Queen's first trip to France, or His Royal Highness the late Duke of Windsor, derailed in Dunkirk docks or Sir Winston Churchill, demanding to board the train from his home at Chartwell. One can imagine that oratorical voice, dec-laring that he would not go up to London to catch it, when the 'Night Ferry' could pick him up at Sevenoaks (Tubs Hill); it did, but the Cus-toms authorities decided that the whole station had to close to every-body else, for the performance! This is easier to understand at the time of writing, for, the Customs are almost paranoid about nasty foreign trains arriving every quarter of an hour, when the Tunnel opens in 1993, even though there may not be that many at first, as the delays get-ting them ordered and built means that all will not be ready immediately.

'For the last time' boomed the station announcer once more, 'the 'Night Ferry' is about to leave for Paris and Brussels. Would passengers please board the train?' So we stepped through those conveniently inward opening doors that the International Union of Railways abhor on new rolling stock. Oblivious to the television cameras filming our departure from the platform, with people crowding the still open door-way, I busied myself in my cabin with placing the completed forms, passport and ticket in the special envelope provided. Dimly I heard the cacaphony of the suburban trains, sounding their horns in farewell.

Wearing ties and hats – unknown when I travelled in 1977 – the BR attendants pursued their duties under arduous conditions, as every-body seemed to be traversing the lurching corridors. It was quite beyond the SNCF Paris computer to berth our party together, or even in the same cars. Hans Hanenbergh, Editor of the Dutch Railways magazine *Koppelinq*, had produced at his own expense a souvenir photostat of most of the 'Night Ferry's' press write-ups, which was most useful for writing the *Night Ferry* book. BR had its own small souvenir

brochure, with small colour pictures, including views of the then new
Sealink waiting room at Folkestone Harbour, and the Belgian RTM Harbour, and the Belgian RTM Jetfoil that was just about to link Dover with
Ostend. Sealink was of course still part of BR until 1984. 'Are you the
young gentleman from Weymouth?' I asked the smart attendant who
was handing these out. 'How do you know I come from Weymouth?'
came the startled reply.

We traversed Beckenham Junction and Bromley South as I opened
the champagne, concealed from thirsty pressmen in a Wagons-Lits
folding holdall, given to certain illustrious clients in by-gone days.
With commendable foresight, I had bought the 'bubbly' in London, in
half bottles to fit the holders, before reading the *Times* headline of that
morning: 'Farewell to BR's *Fawlty Towers*'.

My next door companions, evidently not *Times* readers – perhaps as
well when one recalls Bernard Levin's views on employees of the gas
industry, expressed therein, were sadly disappointed with the
facilities offered by BR, so I cheered them up with some champagne.
But I had reckoned without the souvenir hunters who had already
made off with most of the glasses; even the special right-angle lever
with box-spanner head, used to adjust the stop-cocks of the heating
system, was not sacrosanct. Whoever could have wanted that?

Past Bickley and Sevenoaks, the lurching was so chronic that the
right angle bend at Tonbridge came and went without specific notice.
We stopped for signals only once, at Headcorn, where in the eerie dark
there seemed to be a shadowy Kent and East Sussex train at what had
once been the bay platform, headed by Stroudley 'Terrier' No.3,
though in reality this engine and the coaches were safely slumbering at
nearby Rolvenden, on the operating part of the line.

The sad occasion had its hilarious moments. 'Not quite the *Orient
Express*, is it?' remarked a pressman who could not grasp why any
enthusiast should come all the way from Zurich, to sample the train
before it was taken off. 'Have you ever been on the *Orient Express*?' he
added, blissfully unaware that he was addressing Albert Glatt the
owner of the 'Nostalgie Istanbul Orient Express', already in its fourth
successful year. Nor was the pressman enlightened, though, having
just arrived with the holdall firmly closed, I did not know which way
to look for laughing!!

The 'Venice-Simplon-Orient Express', which runs to a regular timetable, did not then exist, but the Swiss-owned 'Nostalgie Istanbul
Orient Express' which frequently went to Turkey and back, has continued its programme of chartered journeys for the last sixteen years.
It visited every country in Europe except Britain, Spain and Portugal.
In 1992 its excursions, to Kallingrad, in Baltic Russia, for Germans
wishing to visit East Prussia again, especially Konigsberg as the place
is called in German, have been a particular success, and in 1988 the
train made an epic journey from Paris to Hong Kong.

After a very short pause at Dover Western Docks, the '09' shunting engine removed us to the 'Ferry' sidings by the entrance to the now closed Ferry dock. It was extremely slow in stabling the brake, before depositing us, in two portions, aboard the train ferry *St Germain*, by then thirty years old and soon to be withdrawn. A forgotten pleasure was that you were permitted to alight from the sleepers and go on deck. Shortages of deck space for wagons was supposed to be one reason for shutting down the 'Night Ferry', yet only a few days earlier I saw the train ferry *Vortigern* on the ordinary Calais-Folkestone service. We were regaled on deck with a calm, beautiful cloudless night, mild for November. My chief recollection is of incredulity of never being able to go to Paris by through sleeper again this way. Twelve years have gone by, the Tunnel is ready in 1993 but the sleeping cars are not. Why? Because Sir Leon Brittan, EC Commissioner for Competition in 1992, held up the sleeping car service which was to be run jointly by the five railway administrations of Britain, Germany, Netherlands, Belgium and France on the grounds that this was a monopoly. The Railway chiefs are under attack on all sides, from the UK Government which cannot stomach UK railways and really wanted a road tunnel, from the security chiefs who are certain terrorists will cause tunnel fires, and are constantly changing their requirements, and from the County of Kent, which detests the Tunnel and does not seem to want to embrace the opportunities which the opening of the Tunnel will bring. So UK road traffic will greatly increase, instead of transferring to rail for the journey into Europe.

Following a good sleep and an effortless removal from the *St Germain* up the long ramp, seventeen bogie match trucks away from the SNCF diesel shunting engine on the shore, unfortunately I fell asleep again at Dunkirk West. failing to wake until we started from Dunkirk Ville (Town) behind Bo Bo electric 16057 from La Chapelle shed (Paris). Thus I never saw the departure of the last train to Lille, taken off once there were no through sleeping cars to haul. It took away Car No.84 and No.584 of our train, respectively sleepers 3803 and 3794, ending twenty-three years of service between London and Brussels. Ray Privett the young man from Weymouth, woke me with the last cup of 'Travellers Fare' tea to be served on French Railways. My sleeper 3802 seemed to run very well on SNCFs track, which had recently been relaid for 160 kilometres an hour (100 miles an hour) running. I suspect we exceeded the 140 kilometres an hour limit of our sleepers, one of the reasons for taking off the train (though Mark III BR sleepers can and do run at 100 miles an hour). We entered the Gare du Nord at Paris some ten minutes late.

The French engine had no headboard, and SNCF provided no welcoming delegation of officials, though there was something notably absent at Victoria, a porter with a barrow. Hordes of ordinary passengers swept past the sleepers, unaware that they would never see them again on their train from Dunkirk. The Car Nos. were 81 (3983), 82 (3802), 83 (3985), 583 (3797) and 683 (3805). In 1965 3985 ran the London-Basle service. The 3801, now preserved on the 'Bluebell Railway', was in the last train to London, returning empty on the night of 1st-2nd November.

Our party had its own welcome, from the then Director of the French National Railway Museum at Mulhouse, Monsieur Michel Doerr, Maurice Mertens of Railphot, (a consortium of top railway photographers), and indestructable as ever, veteran Wagons-Lits conductor Roger Commault, who turned into another excellent photographer, in retirement after fifty years service. Here he was, photographing the end of the only Paris service of Wagons-Lits that he never conducted, as he did not speak English. Sadly, it was the last time I saw him, for he died in 1981.

We repaired to breakfast in the *Hotel Terminus Nord*, once owned by the Nord Railway. One Dutchman, one Swiss, four French and four English, our ensemble seemed suitably cosmopolitan to be worthy of 'La Maison' as those who enjoyed working for it, often called Wagons-Lits. So ended the Southern's last named train, after forty-four years of through London-Paris train service, without a change of carriage.

Chapter Fifteen

A Hundred Years of Refreshment

It was on the initiative of the National Railway Museum, York, that the Centenary Train of 1979, to mark the Hundred Years of Refreshment on board Britain's railways, became reality. The first dining car began operating in 1879 running between Leeds and London Kings Cross on the Great Northern Railway. It belonged to and was run by the Pullman Palace Car Company (Europe), a division of George M. Pullman's Pullman Palace Car Company which operated some seven thousand Pullmans in America at the time.

The GNR would never have had any 'nasty' Pullman cars, were it not for the Midland Railway competition. Under the MR's fifteen year contract with Pullman, they had twenty parlour cars, and were obliged to haul them about, mostly empty. None were turned into diners until 1882.

The Centenary train was marvellously organized by David Jenkinson, then the NRM's education officer. The Museum did not confine itself to a re-enactment of the Leeds-London run with the press, who were more concerned with the arrival time than with the elegant facilities on board. They ran the train, made up of various preserved coaches from the Museum, all over the country for a week.

Among the tours was an SR one from Southampton to Southampton via Havant, Guildford, Reading and Basingstoke. In 1979 few trains ran along the top of the triangular junction at Havant to or from Southampton.

This was a Pullman occasion. Although vintage LNWR diners were provided, I opted for NRM's Pullman *Eagle*, one of two 1960 cars which they have preserved, and use for their Club. This Club gives York people the chance to go on all kinds of excursions, usually linked to some special preservation project. In this, the Friends of the National Railway Museum often help. They get free entrance to the Museum, so it is well worth joining if you can manage it. There is a colossal Library which I have never properly explored. In the days when books on railways were not so widely available as they are now, you had to ask people on the ground for information. Some amusing stories can only come to hand with retirement. BR employees are like civil servants, not allowed to answer back. That great railwayman, Gerard Fiennes, was dismissed for doing so. Some people are dogmatic. They are right and you are wrong, but with Pullman history, the only thing you can be ninety-nine per cent certain of, is that there are two versions to absolutely everything, and if records in USA say the same thing as in UK, how extremely fortunate. Even the Torquay Pullman fiasco has a version that the GWR Chairman wanted the service, and the General Manager did not, but that hardly accounts for the subsequent facts after the latter had been forced to depart.

Presentation of the Centenary Train was magnificent. BR produced a Train Manager such as were only provided for 'Royal Trains' in 1979, as he did not omit to tell us. All the Pullman opulence was there, the Pullman ambience too, easy going yet the best. We stopped four times just to change the driver, at Fareham, Havant, Guildford and Reading, though the whole journey cannot have been much more than 120 miles and within a fifty mile radius of Southampton, or so, I would hazard a guess. With its electric multiple unit mentality, the Southern Region had no proper engine in 1979 for a train like this. A Class 47 was provided which worked perfectly, despite so many drivers. Much more reliable, fourteen years ago than now, obviously, but of course the engine came . . . from Old Oak Common!

Mr Jenkinson and all the 'Travellers Fare' staff, lived in staff sleepers incorporated in the train, heavy Mark Is in those days, and some even more vintage as far as I recall. But NRM had their own small piece of mystique that always adds spice to a luxury railway journey. For when I entered the Pullman I was staggered to receive a welcome from the Keeper of the Museum himself, Dr Coiley, now retired, flanked by the Librarian Mr Atkins, Mr Edgington and others. It was a wonderful opportunity to meet all these people from York, which they think is an easy place to reach in two hours from Kings Cross, but far from my stamping ground and even further from my present home.

Apparently the NRM had asked the elite of the National Motor Museum at Beaulieu to a private celebratory luncheon excursion, consequently nearly all the top brass of the NRM were already on board the train. Not wishing to deprive the public of a chance to travel in superb 19th century comfort, for dinner they were all ensconced in the 1960 Pullman. So I had an added bonus, and all too soon had made my first and only trip from St Denys to Fareham.

While we waited at Fareham for our first new driver who knew the way to Havant without going to Portsmouth, through eyes half closed from excitement, somehow it was easy to imagine an irate sepulchral Guard who could not wait before setting off in his ghost train up the Meon Valley line. And surely the Fireman was driving the engine at the back, because Mr Drummond's auto arrangements did not work properly? I always believed this to be so, but don't knock the Southern, otherwise it will be said I have a bias in favour of the GWR for suggesting that the GWR Rail Motor Cars were much better than auto-trains though they appeared to be much more similar than their respective names. Just as I was completing this book, there was a letter in the *Railway Magazine* from a retired SR fireman who said precisely this. All the driver did was send bell signals. It must have been somewhat alarming, hurtling along, knowing you could not stop the train with the brake valve under your hand, if you met an adverse signal while 'driving' from the carriage end of the auto-train!

SR Westinghouse brakes seem to have been somewhat temperamental. John Price who for years used the Southern Electric every day from Norwood to London, has a 1974 tale of the Caterham branch set whose first journey of the day started with a tea making ceremony at Caterham. Driver and guard took turns to make the tea, but one morning the brakes leaked while they were enjoying it in the staff room. Luckily the signalman saw it go but as it is down hill all the way to East Croydon, it had to be let out onto the main line at Purley. It went through East Croydon at twenty miles an hour, although it had slowed up somewhat. But the man who had volunteered to join the train at East Croydon and stop it, decided the speed was too great to risk it, so it proceeded unattended to Norwood Junction where it was diverted into the bay, coming to grief, with no casualties to people, luckily.

It was a rare thrill to go from Fareham to Havant avoiding Portsmouth, though now electric trains run hourly over the line from Southampton to Victoria, via Hove and Gatwick Airport, following electrification of the triangle and the line from Portsmouth to Fareham, Eastleigh, and Southampton. In pre war days the Southern ran specials from Victoria's Platform 17, adjoining the Imperial Airways terminal to Berth 50 at Southampton Docks, which was reserved for Imperial Airway's Empire Flying Boats. These trains were made up of four to five vehicles, including one or two Pullmans, and were often hauled by 'T9' 4-4-0s. How sensible of Network South East to remove these artificial barriers which for so long invited passengers to buy a motor car. Changing trains is a hazard of unreliable connections, not because of behaviour like Meon Valley Line guards, but because of late running and cancellations.

I was struck by the 'Travellers Fare' Menu – no mention of Pullman, naturally. After six days on board, serving top class luncheons and dinners every day from several kitchens, with everything cooked on board, the impeccable elegance was most impressive. We had left Southampton at 17.30, aperitifs served en route to Fareham, soup to enjoy during the Havant stop for another driver, the roast beef and three vegetables served with aplomb near Haslemere. The Conductor served the entrée himself in traditional manner to the passengers in the Pullman, despite being in overall charge of all the dining cars on the train.

As we tucked into the roast beef and Yorkshire pudding, Britain's

The Down 'Bournemouth Belle' then Sundays only, near Hook in July 1931, powered by 'Lord Nelson' class 4-6-0 No. 865 *Sir John Hawkins*. *M. W. Earley*

The SR's cross channel steamer *St Briac*, used on the Southampton to St. Malo Service. *J. H. Price Collection*

Britannia Pacific 70009 *Alfred the Lord Tennyson*, Salisbury, 1951. M. W. Earley

A classic picture of a classic train, taken by one of Britain's finest railway photographers, Maurice Earley. Rebuilt Bulleid 'Merchant Navy' Pacific No. 35017 *Belgian Marine* at Worting Junction just south of Basingstoke, on the Down 'Bournemouth Belle' in the summer of 1957.

Stroudley 'Terrier' 0-6-0T No. 32662 crossing the *River Ouse* at Newhaven. As well as being the only access to the railway lines on the west side of the harbour, this bridge carried the main Brighton to Eastbourne Road, at this time, 19th April 1958. *S. C. Nash*

Hastings 1066 line 'DEMU' No. 1105 leads a service out of Mountfield tunnel on 12th April 1974. The restricted clearance in this tunnel was the reason that stock built to the normal loading gauge could not be used on this line. *J. H. Price*

One of Marsh's LB&SCR 'H2' class 'Atlantics' No. 32426, *St Alban's Head*, seen on a special train at Horsted Keynes on 14th August 1955. These locomotives were regular performers on the Newhaven boat trains. Horsted Keynes was soon to find fame as part of the 'Bluebell Line'. *J. H. Price*

Eastbourne in LB&SCR days, with 'I3' class 4-4-2T No. 19 in evidence. *J. H. Price Collection*

For many weary Medloc travellers the Folkestone Harbour branch provided the first sight of home for many years. Here, two of the 'R1' 0-6-0Ts, which worked the branch head a train Up 'the tramroad' on 19th August 1955. Another pair of engines are round the corner out of sight, banking the train. *C. C. Thornburn*

On 15th July 1949 ex SER 'R1s' 0-6-0Ts Nos 1107 and 1337 and ex LCDR 'R1' 0-4-4T head a boat train across the viaduct over Folkestone inner harbour. *L. Hanson*

'4-COR' units at Portsmouth Harbour in the early 1950s. *W. H. Butler Collection*

'U' class Mogul No. 31808 at Portsmouth Harbour. This was a 1928 rebuild of one of the 'Rolling Rivers', 2-6-4Ts. *W. H. Butler Collection*

'A1X Terrier' No.32677 at Hayling Island on 16th September 1956. *J. H. Price*

Compare this 1930's picture of W12 *Ventnor* in Southern livery at Ryde with the last picture in this section. Built in 1880, this engine was originally LBSCR No. 84 *Crowborough*. It went to the Island in November 1903. *W. H. Butler Collection*

'All sorts of steam and a terrific smell of the sea'. W22 *Brading* about to leave Ryde Esplanade for the Pier Head, 8th August 1964. *J. H. Price*

'O2' class W14 *Fishbourne* at Cowes, 8th August 1964. *J. H. Price*

The now preserved 'O2' class W24 *Calbourne*, enters Brading in 1953. *W. H. Butler Collection*

'O2' class W14 *Fishbourne* at Brading in 1953. *W. H. Butler Collection*

One of the ex-London Transport tube trains arrives on the Island on the Fishbourne ferry *Camber Queen*. *F. E. J. Ward*

Above: The Channel Islands boat train edges its way along the tramway at Weymouth passing the Bistro cafe and cargo platform, 16th July 1972.

J. H. Price

On the Isle of Wight Steam Railway a pair of Stroudley 'Terriers' have been restored in the liveries of two of the Island's original railway companies, the Freshwater, Yarmouth, Newport and the Isle of Wight Central Railway. *Isle of Wight Steam Railway*

national dish, loudspeakers told envious travellers on the platform at Guildford not to board, as this was a special. This careful attention to passengers always gives me an extra kick when in a BR special – well, I told you pages ago that perhaps I have the wrong sort of sense of humour.

This was the way to travel. In those days of the late '70s, British Rail was doing everything possible to stop the 'Venice-Simplon-Orient Express' from setting a precedent for using non-BR rolling stock on its lines. The NRM's effort seemed to me something of a breakthrough, though of course it was a BR celebration, and therefore a BR train doing the celebrating with NRM's coaches, for which special dispensation had been graciously granted. It was now practically dark, and how pleasant to sail slowly and majestically non-stop through sad semi-military stations like North Camp, enjoying 'Travellers Fare' claret with the repast.

Now the Sherry trifle came, elegantly served, and when I asked for a glass of water with it, a whole jug was placed on the table. That had not happened for years. There seemed to be a lot of half-forgotten finishing touches to the service of this excellent dinner, that were not just nostalgic, but eerily familiar. Who, I asked the knowlegeable VIPs of the National Railway Museum, was this wonderful Pullman Conductor, now in 'Travellers Fare' employ, who produced all this, so in keeping with all that is set out in my book *Pullman in Europe*? There was an awkward pause. Then it was rather grudgingly disclosed that the Conductor in charge of all the dining on the train, was not in fact ever in the Pullman Car Company's service, but was a senior Western Region Conductor from South Wales.

We rumbled over the double junction points outside Reading, used by through trains to reach the down Great Western main line to Bristol, South Wales and the West, while the Southern Electrics continued to use the ramp, which now leads into what was the bay of the Down main Reading General platform at its Up end, once reserved for the station pilot and the postmen, when mail had to be transferred by electric truck to the long demolished SR station next door.

We paused, lengthily, at Reading's Down main platform, while we waited for the driver who knew the Basingstoke branch and the Southern main line to Southampton, on the only piece of the old 6 pm Paddington-Weymouth Express route which we would follow, though only to nearby Southcote Junction, beyond Reading West. The Conductor served the cheese in deferential silence, as though he knew, much better than these eminent historians from York who were his passengers, how these things ought to be done.

Perhaps it was the water jug, perhaps the celery (the Menu said 'Salad'), long sticks in a vase. Perhaps it was the ex-GWR track, or maybe it was the claret. Above all it was the assured modesty of perfect presentation, that reminded me of so many journeys with my late brother-in-law, the actor Elwyn Brook Jones, when travelling non-stop from Paddington to Newbury in Phil Metcalfe's 6 pm GWR Weymouth dining car, which he ran for twenty years or more, before ending his career on the 'Cornish Riviera Express'. As we waited in Reading – I shudder to think how many hours I must have wasted in all the times I have waited in GWR trains at Reading, nostalgic curiosity overcame me. When the Conductor brought round more biscuits, not of course, railway assortment, even Huntley and Palmers was soon to disappear, their superior Reading biscuits taken over by the American Nabisco, I asked him if he had ever encountered an elderly GWR conductor named Metcalfe? The Conductor gave me a long, penetrating look, as if quizzically trying to recall whom this passenger was, whose treatment by the NRM VIPs was so courteous, even respectful.

Then he said, very slowly: 'I was Phil Metcalfe's pantry boy'.

Appendix A

Preserved SR Locomotives

The most up to date listing of preserved SR locomotives is that published in *Steam Railway* in November 1992 and reproduced here with the kind permission of the editor Nigel Harris.

Of eighty-six Southern locomotives, two have distinguished main line careers in preservation (Nos. 34092 and 35028) but are now withdrawn for major repair. We hope their absence is only temporary.

Including No. 35029, there are twelve static exhibits which at present are not intended for restoration to working order. An encouraging total of twenty-two locomotives are in traffic, with four more likely to return to work before next season.

Those locomotives not yet restored to working order number twenty-two. The figure for locomotives which have operated but are now withdrawn for overhaul is twenty-five. The preservation movement clearly has plenty to keep it busy for a long time!

No. W24 *Calbourne* 'O2' 0-4-4T: The only survivor of the Isle of Wight's Class O2 0-4-4Ts is based on the Isle of Wight Steam Railway at Haven Street. Currently being dismantled for 10-year boiler examination.

No. 82 *Boxhill* 'A1' 0-6-0T: Part of the national Railway Museum collection, restored for static display in the museum's inter-active educational section.

No. B110 'E1' 0-6-0T: This locomotive was acquired for preservation from a colliery in 1963, never having been part of BR stock. Preserved at Chasewater, it was never steamed in preservation, and moved to the East Somerset Railway, for restoration. Work has recently been completed, the locomotive has been steamed, and will be finished as SR No. B110.

No. 563 'T3' 4-4-0: Part of the National Railway Museum collection, restored for static display.

No. B618 *Gladstone* 0-4-2: The famous LBSCR 0-4-2 was acquired for preservation by the Stephenson Locomotive Society and passed in due course to the National Railway Museum collection. It is restored for static display.

No. DS680 *Waddon* 'A1' 0-6-0T: This Brighton 'Terrier' was exported to Canada in the late 1960s together with Gresley 'A4' 4-6-2 No. 60010 *Dominion of Canada* for museum display in Delson, Quebec.

No. 30053 'M7' 0-4-4T: After withdrawal by BR, No. 30053 spent more than 20 years in the USA, on display at Steamtown in Vermont. It was repatriated to the UK two years ago and has recently been restored to traffic at the East Anglia Railway Museum, operating over BR lines around Salisbury before being returned to its 'base' on the Swanage Railway.

No. 30064 'USA' 0-6-0T: One of the SR's 'USA' dock tanks acquired from BR service by the Bluebell Railway. Although part of the operational fleet for many years, it is currently out of traffic awaiting repairs but is stored complete.

No. 30065 'USA' 0-6-0T: One of the two 'USA' tanks obtained by the Kent & East Sussex Railway from BR departmental service. No. 30065 is currently undergoing overhaul.

No. 30070 'USA' 0-6-0T: No. 30070 is also dismantled for overhaul at Rolvenden on the Kent & East Sussex Railway.

No. 30072 'USA' 0-6-0T: A long-time stalwart of the working fleet on the Keighley & Worth Valley Railway, No. 30072 is currently in Oxenhope Museum awaiting removal to Haworth for investigation of a leaking stay.

No. 30075 'USA' 0-6-0T: A real interloper is No. 30075, since it never ran in the UK. It is a 'USA' built in Yugoslavia, purchased out of traffic from that country and restored at the Swanage Railway to represent an addition to the ranks of the genuine SR locomotives. It entered traffic at Swanage in 1992.

No. 30096 'B4' 0-4-0T: Restored to working order on the Bluebell Railway and currently part of the operating fleet.

No. 30102 'B4' 0-4-0T: Cosmetically restored and on static display at the Bressingham Steam Museum, Norfolk.

No. 30120 'T9' 4-4-0: No. 30120 is part of the National Collection and is currently on loan to the Swanage Railway. It is permitted only a limited number of days in steam until withdrawal for overhaul in 1993. It is then likely to be restored to main line operating condition.

No. 30245 'M7' 0-4-4T: Cosmetically restored for display purposes. Part of the National Railway Museum collection.

No. 30499 'S15' 4-6-0: Stored in ex-Barry condition at the Mid-Hants Railway. Its tender is to be rebuilt first.

No. 30506 'S15' 4-6-0: Another ex-Barry 'S15', this one is currently in traffic on the Mid-Hants Railway.

No. 30541 'Q' 0-6-0: Restored to working order at the Bluebell Railway but currently out of traffic awaiting overhaul.

No. 30583 '0415' 4-4-2T: Acquired out of service from BR and a stalwart of the operating fleet at the Bluebell Railway, but currently out of traffic awaiting boiler repairs.

No. 30585 '0298' 2-4-0T: Two of the three then surviving Beattie well tanks were acquired for preservation direct from BR service. No. 30585 was operated at Buckinghamshire Railway Centre, but has been out of traffic for some years. Its restoration to working order is now being given priority.

No. 30587: The other preserved Beattie well tank is part of the National Railway Museum collection, and on loan to the South Devon Railway for static display at Buckfastleigh.

No. 30777 *Sir Lamiel* 'N15' 4-6-0: Part of the National Museum collection. Restored to working order by the North Eastern Locomotive Preservation Group at Hull and currently available for main line operation on BR.

No. 30825 'S15' 4-6-0: Broken for spares.

No. 30828 'S15' 4-6-0: Restored to working order on private premises at Eastleigh. Completion imminent.

No. 30830 'S15' 4-6-0: Awaiting restoration at the Bluebell Railway. Currently in ex-Barry condition with no work done.

No. 30841 'S15' 4-6-0: Once named *Greene King* SR No. 841 has been a stalwart of the North Yorkshire Moors Railway fleet for many years. It is currently in traffic.

No. 30847 'S15' 4-6-0: Restoration of No. 30847 from Barry condition is nearing completion at the Bluebell Railway. It is hoped that the 4-6-0 will return to traffic.

No. 30850 *Lord Nelson* 'LN' 4-6-0: Part of the National Railway Museum Collection, No. 850 was restored to working order and operated on BR main line tours, but has since been withdrawn following expiry of its main line 'ticket'.

No. 30925 *Cheltenham* 'V' 4-4-0: Another National Railway Museum engine, No. 30925 was steamed for 'Rocket 150' but has otherwise remained as a static museum exhibit.

No. 30926 *Repton* 'V' 4-4-0: No. 30926 was sold out of traffic to the Steamtown museum in the USA. It was repatriated at the same time as No. 30053 and restored to working order on the North Yorkshire Moors Railway. It was subsequently transferred on loan to the Great Central Railway where it forms part of the operational fleet. It was due to return to the NYMR in February 1993.

No. 30928 *Stowe* 'V' 4-4-0: Originally displayed at the Montagu Motor Museum and later at the East Somerset Railway, No. 30928 was restored at the Bluebell Railway. It is currently out of traffic awaiting a 10-year overhaul.

No. 31027 'P' 0-6-0T: One of the Bluebell Railway's early working fleet, No. 31027 is dismantled for overhaul.

No. 31065 'O1' 0-6-0: Initially preserved at Ashford Steam Centre, when the centre closed this locomotive was moved to a private site Kent. It is not accessible to the public and has been dismantled. A loss to preservation.

No. 31156 'P' 0-6-0T: This 'P' class 0-6-0T preserved on the East & Kent Sussex Railway, was acquired from a local flour mill where it had been operated as a private shunter. It is currently in traffic.

No. 31178 'P' 0-6-0T: One of three 'P' tanks owned by the Bluebell Railway, No. 31178 is dismantled for restoration.

No. 31232 'P' 0-6-0T: The Bluebell Railway's popular tank named *Bluebell* is currently part of the operating fleet.

No. 31263 'H' 0-4-4T: Acquired out of BR service for the abortive Hawkhurst branch preservation project, No. 263 was restored at Robertsbridge before passing to the Bluebell Railway. It is currently part of the traffic fleet.

No. 31592 'C' 0-6-0: Another stalwart member of the Bluebell Railway working fleet, this locomotive is about to be admitted to works and dismantled for 10-year overhaul.

No. 31618 'U' 2-6-0: No. 31618 is in traffic on the Bluebell Railway, Sheffield Park.

No. 31625 'U' 2-6-0: One of several ex-Barry Maunsell 'Moguls' in preservation, No. 31625 is dismantled and undergoing restoration at Ropley, on the Mid-Hants Railway.

No. 31638 'U' 2-6-0: Acquired from Woodhams, Barry scrapyard by the Bluebell Railway but no work yet done.

No. 31737 'D' 4-4-0: Part of the National Railway Museum collection. Restored for static display at the museum in York.

No. 31806 'U' 2-6-0: This locomotive was restored from Barry condition to working order on the Mid-Hants Railway but is now stored out of traffic awaiting overhaul.

No. 31874 'N' 2-6-0: The history of this locomotive is similar to that of No. 31806. No. 31874 was one of the original working locomotives on the Mid-Hants Railway. It is stored awaiting overhaul.

No. 32473 *Birch Grove* 'E4' 0-6-2T: Acquired out of BR service by the Bluebell Railway and much-used in the early years. *Birch Grove* has been out of traffic for many years and is now dismantled for restoration. The chassis is now re-assembled and the boiler is awaiting attention.

No. 32636 'A1X' 0-6-0T: The Bluebell's *Fenchurch*, one of the railway's original working locomotives, is undergoing overhaul. New front wheel castings have been obtained.

No. 32640 'A1X' 0-6-0T: In service as IWC No. 11 *Newport* on the Isle of Wight Steam Railway, Haven Street.

No. 32646 'A1X' 0-6-0T: In service as FYN No. 8 *Freshwater* on the Isle of Wight Steam Railway, Haven Street.

No. 32650 'A1X' 0-6-0T: In service on the Kent & East Sussex Railway as SR No. 50 *Sutton*.

No. 32655 'A1X' 0-6-0T: The Bluebell Railway's *Stepney* is out of traffic awaiting a 10-year overhaul.

No. 32662 'A1X' 0-6-0T: On static display at the Bressingham Steam Museum, Norfolk.

No. 32670 'A1X' 0-6-0T: This 'Terrier' is an original KESR locomotive, No. 3 *Bodiam* dating from independant and BR days. It has worked in preservation but is dismantled, awaiting a decision on either major boiler repairs or a new boiler.

No. 32678 'A1X' 0-6-0T: The third of the 'Terriers' on the Kent & East Sussex Railway was LBSCR No. 78 *Knowle*. It is currently dismantled and awaiting restoration, having been used in service in the early years of the preservation society.

No. 33001 'Q1' 0-6-0: Part of the National Railway Museum collection, Bulleid 'Q1' 0-6-0 has recently been returned to traffic on the Bluebell Railway, Sheffield Park.

No. 34007 *Wadebridge* 'WC' 4-6-2: Moved from the Plym Valley Railway to the Bodmin & Wenford Railway at Bodmin General station, No. 34007 will have been dismantled by the time this appears in print. Work is about to commence on stripping the boiler and wheelsets.

No. 34010 *Sidmouth* Rebuilt 'WC' 4-6-2: Under restoration on a private site in Middlesbrough. No public access.

No. 34016 *Bodmin* Rebuilt 'WC' 4-6-2: No. 34016 was restored to working order on the Mid-Hants Railway. It is currently dismantled for a major overhaul.

No. 34023 *Blackmore Vale* 'WC' 4-6-2: Acquired out of BR service and the first air-smoothed Bulleid to work in preservation. It is awaiting overhaul at the Bluebell Railway.

No. 34027 *Taw Valley* Rebuilt 'WC' 4-6-2: Restored at the North Yorkshire Moors, East Lancashire and Severn Valley Railways, where it is now based. Passed for main line operation and frequently in use on main line tours.

No. 34028 *Eddystone* Rebuilt 'WC' 4-6-2: Restoration work is in progress on a private site at Sellindge, Kent. No public access. A new cab has been fabricated

No. 34039 *Boscastle* Rebuilt 'WC' 4-6-2: Restoration is nearing completion on the Great Central Railway, after 19 years work. It has been given a hydraulic rest and awaits a steam test/final adjustments. Its return to traffic is imminent.

No. 34046 *Braunton* Rebuilt 'WC' 4-6-2: Acquired out of BR service for the National Collection, but has received only cosmetic restoration and is seldom displayed.

No. 34051 *Winston Churchill* 'BB' 4-6-2: Acquired out of BR service for the National Collection, but has received only cosmetic restoration and is seldom displayed.

No. 34053 *Sir Keith Park* Rebuilt 'BB' 4-6-2: Undergoing restoration on a private site. No public access.

No. 34058 *Sir Frederick Pile* Rebuilt 'BB' 4-6-2: Undergoing restoration at the Avon Valley Railway, Bitton. Boiler, frames and wheels are still assembled. A new cab, pipework and many parts have been fabricated and a tender will be built. Work is expected to take another three years.

No. 34059 *Sir Archibald Sinclair* Rebuilt 'BB' 4-6-2: Undergoing restoration at the Bluebell Railway, with a view to completion in about two years time.

No. 34067 *Tangmere* 'BB' 4-6-2: This ex-Barry engine is dismantled for long-term restoration at the MHR.

No. 34070 *Manston* **'BB' 4-6-2:** Under restoration on a private site at Richborough Power Station. No public access.

No. 34072 *257 Squadron* **'BB' 4-6-2:** Restored by the Swanage Railway and currently on loan to the East Lancs. Return to Swanage is imminent.

No. 34073 *249 Squadron* **'BB' 4-6-2:** Acquired for preservation and stored at former BR workshops at Brighton. Not accessible to the public.

No. 34081 *92 Squadron* **'BB' 4-6-2:** Under long-term restoration from Barry condition at the Nene Valley Railway, Wansford. Re-assembly is taking place and materials on hand include boiler tubes and many fittings. The tender is complete but the frame for the air-smoothed casing has yet to be manufactured and other parts remain to be obtained.

No. 34092 *City of Wells* **'WC' 4-6-2:** Preserved at the Keighley & Worth Balley Railway, the Giesl-ejector converted Bullied 'Pacific' has been a very successful main line engine. It is currently dismantled at Haworth for major overhaul.

No. 34101 *Hartland* **Rebuilt 'WC' 4-6-2:** Restoration of this Bulleid 'Pacific' is at an advanced stage at the Great Central Railway. Completion expected Spring '93.

No. 34105 *Swanage* **'WC' 4-6-2:** Restored from Barry condition at the Mid-Hants Railway; in working order.

No. 35005 *Canadian Pacific* **Rebuilt 'MN' 4-6-2:** Restored from Barry condition at Steamtown, Carnforth and later on the Great Central Railway; in working order.

No. 35006 *Peninsula & Oriental SN Co* **Rebuilt 'MN' 4-6-2:** Dismantled at the Gloucester Warwickshire Railway, where it is being restored by the 35006 P&O Locomotive Soc. The chassis is being re-assembled under cover; the boiler is stored at Toddington. Frames and tank have been manufactured for the tender, which is being built from scratch.

No. 35011 *General Steam Navigation* **Rebuilt 'MN' 4-6-2:** Moved from Barry to Brighton where it is stored on an open siding in ex-Barry condition; no public access.

No. 35018 *British India Line* **Rebuilt 'MN' 4-6-2:** The first of the Bulleid 'Pacifics' to be rebuilt by BR in 1956 is partially dismantled at the Mid-Hants Railway. Restoration was commenced but at present progress is halted as the locomotive is over the line's maximum axle weight limit.

No. 35022 *Holland-America Line* **Rebuilt 'MN' 4-6-2:** Stored in ex-Barry condition at the Swanage Railway.

No. 35025 *Brocklebank Line* **Rebuilt 'MN' 4-6-2:** Stored in ex-Barry condition at the Great Central Railway. It is a long-term restoration and as a first step the locomotive will be moved to Loughborough for the boiler to be lifted.

No. 35027 *Port Line* **Rebuilt 'MN' 4-6-2:** Rebuilt from Barry condition at the Bluebell Railway and currently in traffic.

No. 35028 *Clan Line* **Rebuilt 'MN' 4-6-2:** Acquired out of service from BR and maintained at Liss, Ashford and later at Hereford, from where it operated BR main line tours. No.35028 has been a stalwart main line locomotive for some years and is currently undergoing restoration in Flying Scotsman Services private premises at Southall.

No. 35029 *Ellerman Lines* **Rebuilt 'MN' 4-6-2:** No. 35029 is unique among standard gauge locomotives as it forms a sectioned exhibit at the National Railway Museum, York, with parts cut away to show its internal workings. Mounted with its driving wheels slightly off the rails, it can be demonstrated with its wheels rotated by an electric motor.

Appendix B

Headcodes

The Southern has been synonomous with headcodes since the introduction of Electric Multiple units. Originally letters were used, but this caused a certain amount of restriction as new routes were opened up.

Services which can reach a destination via assorted routes will have different headcodes as for example trains via the Quarry line, would have a different code to those travelling via Redhill.

Some selected headcodes more commonly seen are:

South Eastern Division, many of which have come into existence as a result of the Kent Coast electrification. They have changed little over the years.

2 CHARING CROSS TO CANNON STREET Shuttle service common when engineering work takes place.

4 CHARING CROSS TO FOLKESTONE HARBOUR/MARGATE via Orpington.

6 CHARING CROSS TO GROVE PARK SIDINGS, ecs service only.

8 CHARING CROSS TO ASHFORD via Orpington

12 CHARING CROSS TO ORPINGTON

13 CANNON STREET TO ORPINGTON

14 VICTORIA TO FOLKESTONE HARBOUR/ DOVER WESTERN DOCKS via Herne Hill and Bat and Ball.

15 VICTORIA TO FOLKESTONE HARBOUR/ DOVER WESTERN DOCKS via Catford and Bat and Ball.

16 CHARING CROSS TO SEVENOAKS via Orpington.

18 CHARING CROSS TO MARGATE via Orpington, Dover and Minster.

19 CHARING CROSS TO MARGATE via Orpington, Dover and Margate.

20 ASHFORD TO HASTINGS

22 CHARING CROSS TO HASTINGS
via Battle.

23 CANNON STREET TO HASTINGS
via Battle.

24 CHARING CROSS TO HAYES

25 CANNON STREET TO HAYES

26 CHARING CROSS TO ADDISCOMBE

27 CANNON STREET TO ADDISCOMBE

30 CHARING CROSS TO TUNBRIDGE
WELLS via Orpington.

33 CANNON STREET TO TUNBRIDGE
WELLS via Orpington.

40 CHARING CROSS TO DARTFORD
via Sidcup.

41 CANNON STREET TO DARTFORD
via Sidcup.

44 CHARING CROSS TO GRAVESEND/
STROOD via Sidcup.

45 CANNON STREET TO GRAVESEND/
STROOD via Sidcup.

46 VICTORIA TO DOVER WESTERN DOCKS
via Herne Hill and Orpington.

46 CHARING CROSS TO SIDCUP/
SLADE GREEN

47 CANNON STREET TO SIDCUP/
SLADE GREEN

48 VICTORIA TO DOVER WESTERN DOCKS
via Chatham, this applies to boat trains
only and is therefore non stop.

50 CHARING CROSS TO DARTFORD
via Lewisham and Sidcup.

51 CANNON STREET TO DARTFORD
via Lewisham and Sidcup.

56 VICTORIA TO FOLKESTONE HARBOUR
via Herne Hill and Orpington.

60 CHARING CROSS TO DARTFORD
via Lewisham and Erith.

61 CANNON STREET DARTFORD
via Lewisham and Erith.

70 CHARING CROSS TO DARTFORD
via Bexleyheath.

71 CANNON STREET TO DARTFORD
via Bexleyheath.

72 VICTORIA TO ORPINGTON
via Catford.

74 VICTORIA TO DOVER WESTERN DOCKS
via Herne Hill and Chatham.

80 CHARING CROSS TO DARTFORD
via Greenwich.

81 CANNON STREET TO DARTFORD
via Greenwich.

01 GROVE PARK TO BROMLEY NORTH

00 CANNON STREET TO BLACKFRIARS/
ST. PAULS

07 VICTORIA TO ST. PAULS

Central Division, the codes on this division underwent a major change in the mid 70's and most have been renumbered, old codes in brackets. The code that is best remembered and been in existence since 1933 is 4.

0 ALL POINTS TO NEW CROSS GATE
ecs only.

14 VICTORIA TO BRIGHTON
semi fast, via Quarry. (12)

1 PURLEY TO TATTENHAM CORNER

15 LONDON BRIDGE TO BRIGHTON
semi fast, via Quarry. (13)

2 WIMBLEDON TO WEST CROYDON
via Mitcham. (2)

16 VICTORIA TO BOGNOR REGIS
via Redhill and Horsham. (98)

2 VICTORIA TO LITTLEHAMPTON
via Quarry and Hove. (16)

20 VICTORIA TO GATWICK AIRPORT
via Quarry.

3 LONDON BRIDGE TO LITTLEHAMPTON
via Quarry and Hove.

23 LONDON BRIDGE TO GUILDFORD
via Brockley and Sutton.

4 VICTORIA TO BRIGHTON
via Quarry, maximum of two stops.

30 VICTORIA TO GATWICK AIRPORT
via Redhill.

5 OXTED TO UCKFIELD

32 VICTORIA TO LITTLEHAMPTON/
BOGNOR via Redhill and Horsham. (98)

8 VICTORIA TO PORTSMOUTH HARBOUR
via Quarry and Horsham.

34 VICTORIA TO BRIGHTON
semi fast, via Redhill.

10 VICTORIA TO REDHILL/REIGATE

35 LONDON BRIDGE TO BRIGHTON
semi fast, via Redhill.

11 LONDON BRIDGE TO REDHILL/REIGATE
via Brockley.

42 BRIGHTON TO SEAFORD

43 BRIGHTON TO LEWES/EASTBOURNE

44 VICTORIA TO BRIGHTON
stopping service.

45 LONDON BRIDGE TO BRIGHTON
stopping service.

46 VICTORIA TO SOUTHAMPTON
via Quarry and Hove.

50 VICTORIA TO EASTBOURE
via Quarry. (52)

51 LONDON BRIDGE TO EASTBOURNE
via Quarry

52 VICTORIA TO NEWHAVEN
via Quarry. (76)

60 BRIGHTON TO PORTSMOUTH
HARBOUR semi fast service.

62 BRIGHTON TO PORTSMOUTH
HARBOUR stopping service.

64 BRIGHTON TO LITTLEHAMPTON

65 BRIGHTON TO WEST WORTHING

66 VICTORIA TO EAST GRINSTEAD

67 LITTLEHAMPTON/BARNHAM TO
BOGNOR

68 VICTORIA TO WEST SUTTON
via West Croydon.

72 VICTORIA TO EAST CROYDON/
TATTENHAM CORNER stopping service.

74 VICTORIA TO TATTENHAM CORNER
via Selhurst.

83 PURLEY TO CATERHAM

84 VICTORIA TO EPSOM/BOGNOR
via Mitcham Junction.
(40 for Bognor services)

86 VICTORIA TO BECKENHAM JUNCTION

88 VICTORIA TO UCKFIELD. (60)

96 VICTORIA TO EPSOM DOWNS
via Mitcham Junction.

99 LONDON BRIDGE TO UCKFIELD

05 LONDON BRIDGE TO STREATHAM
HILL, ecs only.

South Western Division, the founder of train headcodes, although originally only letters were used. May have since come into existence with the electrification of the Bournemouth, Weymouth and Fareham electrification schemes.

5 WATERLOO TO SOUTHAMPTON
via Havant and Netley.

7 WATERLOO TO EASTLEIGH
via Havant and Botley.

10 WATERLOO TO WOKING

13 WATERLOO TO WATERLOO
via Weybridge and Brentford.

14 WATERLOO TO WATERLOO
via Weybridge and Richmond.

16 WATERLOO TO EFFINGHAM
JUNCTION/GUILDFORD via Epsom.

17 WATERLOO TO DORKING

18 WATERLOO TO CHESSINGTON SOUTH

19 WATERLOO TO EPSOM/LEATHERHEAD

20 CLAPHAM JUNCTION TO KENSINGTON
OLYMPIA

24 WATERLOO TO SHEPPERTON
via Earlsfield.

30 WATERLOO TO HAMPTON COURT

32 WATERLOO TO WATERLOO
via Richmond and Kingston.

36 WATERLOO TO READING
via Richmond and Ascot.

37 WATERLOO TO READING
via Brentford fast.

42 WATERLOO TO EFFINGHAM
JUNCTION/GUILDFORD via Cobham.

44 EASTLEIGH TO BRISTOL

47 WATERLOO TO SHEPPERTON
via Richmond.

51 WATERLOO TO ALTON
fast.

52 WATERLOO TO ALTON
semi fast.

53 WATERLOO TO ALTON
slow.

58 WATERLOO TO WINDSOR
via Richmond.

62 WATERLOO TO BASINGSTOKE/ SALISBURY/EXETER ST. DAVIDS

86 WATERLOO TO WIMBLEDON via East Putney.

66 READING TO BASINGSTOKE/ SALISBURY/EXETER ST. DAVIDS

91 WATERLOO TO EASTLEIGH/ WEYMOUTH fast service.

68 WATERLOO TO KINGSTON via Richmond.

92 WATERLOO TO EASTLEIGH/ WEYMOUTH semi fast service.

75 WATERLOO TO GUILDFORD via Worplesdon.

93 WATERLOO TO EASTLEIGH/ WEYMOUTH stopping service.

80 WATERLOO TO PORTSMOUTH HARBOUR via Eastleigh.

95 WATERLOO TO SOUTHAMPTON EASTERN DOCKS

81 WATERLOO TO PORTSMOUTH HARBOUR via Worplesdon fast service.

96 WATERLOO TO SOUTHAMPTON WESTERN DOCKS

82 WATERLOO TO PORTSMOUTH HARBOUR via Worplesdon semi fast service.

97 WATERLOO/BROCKENHURST TO LYMINGTON PIER

83 WATERLOO TO PORTSMOUTH HARBOUR via Worplesdon stopping service.

03 WATERLOO TO WIMBLEDON DEPOT via East Putney.

85 PORTSMOUTH HARBOUR TO SOUTHAMPTON

The introduction of Thameslink introduced many new codes.

3 THAMESLINK TO BECKENHAM JUNCTION

17 THAMESLINK TO ORPINGTON/ SEVENOAKS

9 THAMESLINK TO BELLINGHAM.

22 THAMESLINK TO HAYES

13 THAMESLINK TO PURLEY via Herne Hill, Tulse Hill and Selhurst.

25 THAMESLINK TO SUTTON via Herne Hill and Selhurst.

28	**THAMESLINK TO BRIGHTON** via Brockley and Quarry.
29	**THAMESLINK TO BRIGHTON** via Brockley and Redhill.
31	**THAMESLINK TO WIMBLEDON** via Herne Hill, Mitcham Junction and West Sutton.
37	**THAMESLINK TO SUTTON** via Herne Hill and St. Helier.
42	**THAMESLINK TO PURLEY** via Herne Hill and Crystal Palace.
43	**THAMESLINK TO GUILDFORD** via Herne Hill, Selhurst and Sutton.
61	**THAMESLINK TO SWANLEY** via Herne Hill and St. Mary Cray.
71	**THAMESLINK TO ORPINGTON** via Herne Hill.
75	**THAMESLINK TO HERNE HILL**

This information has been supplied to the publishers by the Southern Electric Group which was formed in 1970 and exists to promote interest in the electric railway system of the Southern Region and its successors. It publishes a bi-monthly magazine, *Live Rail* to members. Through an associated company – SEG (Preservation) Ltd – the Group has preserved Southern Railway built '4 COR' No. 3142 which is undergoing restoration and is the only complete ex-main line electric multiple unit in preservation. Full details and membership of the Southern Electric Group can be obtained from 12 Dorchester Gardens, Grand Avenue, Worthing, West Sussex, BN11 5AY.

Appendix C

Southern Logos and Advertisements

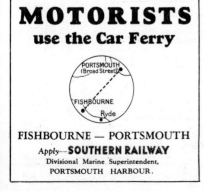

SOUTHERN RAILWAY

REG. DU COMM. : SEINE No. 209.639.

CONTINENTAL SERVICES

INCLUDING THE

CHANNEL ISLANDS

OCTOBER 4th, 1936, and until further notice.

Every exertion is made to secure the punctuality of the trains and boats, but their arrival or departure at the times stated will not be guaranteed ; nor will the Company be responsible for delay, or any consequences arising therefrom, whether caused by the state of the weather, the tide, or otherwise, nor for the information given as regards the trains of other Railway and Steamship Companies, or Administrations.

SUMMARY OF CONTENTS.

RAILWAY MAP OF EUROPE
and connections with Near East at end of book.

G.W.R., L.&N.E.R. AND L.M.&S.R. STATIONS
TO THE CONTINENT VIA SOUTHERN
RAILWAY.

For full particulars see pages 113 and 114.

AT YOUR SERVICE!

For information, Tickets, etc., write or call :—
CONTINENTAL ENQUIRY OFFICE,
Victoria Station, London, S.W.I.

THE SUMMER EDITION OF THIS HANDBOOK WILL BE PUBLISHED IN MAY, 1937.

(See announcement on page 30 regarding altered time-tables from April 4th, 1937).

Appendix E

Isle of Wight and Continental Connections

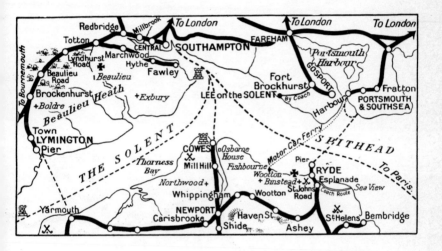

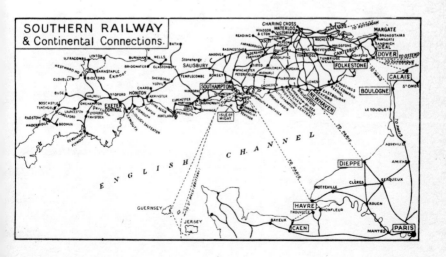

Appendix F

SR in the Isle of Wight

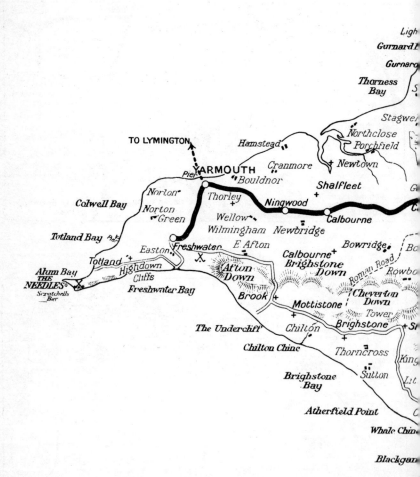

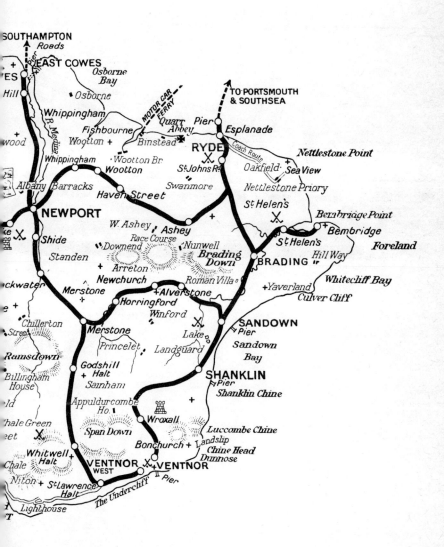

Appendix G

Southampton Docks Rail Network
circa 1960

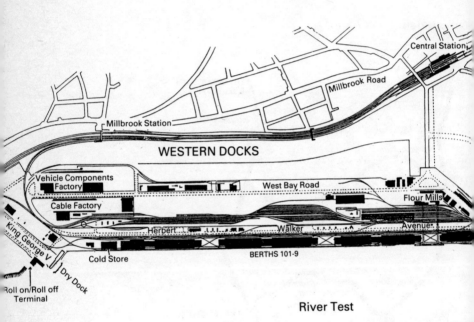

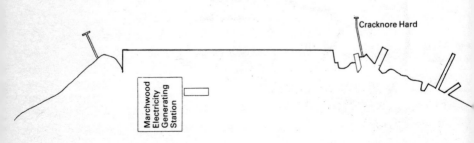

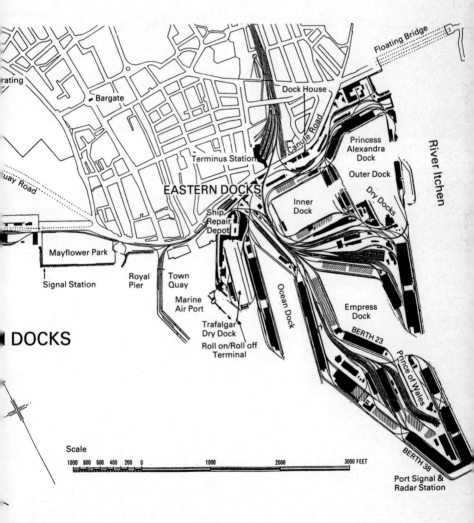

Appendix H

Southern Railway's Network

See fold out map at the end of the book.

Appendix I

Southern Electric Suburban Network

See fold out map at the end of the book.

Bibliography

Channel Islands Railway Steamers: K. le Scelleur; Patrick Stephens, 1984.
Dream Voyages – Concorde, QE2, Venice-Simplon-Orient Express:
  Gary C. Buchanan B SC, FRGS; Jersey Artists, 1989
History of the Southern Railway: C. F. Dendy Marshall, Revised
  R. W. Kidner 1988; Ian Allan, 1988.
Jersey Airlines International: George Behrend; Jersey Artists,
  2nd Impression, 1972.
Night Ferry: George Behrend & Gary Buchanan; Jersey Artists, 1985.
On and Off the Rails: Sir John Elliot; Allen & Unwin, London, 1982.
Pullman: Julian Morel; David & Charles, 1983.
Pullman in Europe: George Behrend; Ian Allan, 1962.
Sir Herbert Walker's Southern Railway: Charles F. Klapper; Routledge &
  Keegan Paul, 1975.
Southampton's Railways: Bert Moody; Waterfront Publications (Poole),
  1992.
Southern Electric, 1909-79: G. T. Moody; 9th edition, Ian Allan, 1979.
Southern Railway Branch Lines (Locomotion Papers No. 95): R. W. Kidner;
  Oakwood Press, 1976.
The Colonel Stephens Railways: John Scott Morgan; David & Charles,
  4th Impression, 1992.
The History of the Southern Railway: Dr Michael R. Bonavia MA Ph D
  MCIT; Unwin Hyman, 1987.
The London Chatham & Dover Railway: R. W. Kidner; Oakwood Press.
The South Eastern & Chatham Railway: R. W. Kidner; Oakwood Press.
The Southern Railway: R. W. Kidner; Oakwood Press.
The Waterloo & Southampton Line (Locomotion Papers No. 140):
  R. W. Kidner; Oakwood Press, 1983.

Index

Note numbers in *italic* refer to illustrations and maps